Other titles in the A Retreat With... *Series:*

A Retreat With Mark: Embracing Discipleship,
by Stephen C. Doyle, O.F.M.

A Retreat With Mary of Magdala and Augustine:
Rejoicing in Human Sexuality, by Sidney Callahan

A Retreat With Oscar Romero and Dorothy Day:
Walking With the Poor, by Marie Dennis

A Retreat With Our Lady, Dominic and Ignatius:
Praying With Our Bodies, by Betsey Beckman,
Nina O'Connor and J. Michael Sparough, S.J.

A Retreat With Our Lady of Guadalupe and Juan Diego:
Heeding the Call, by Virgilio Elizondo and Friends

A Retreat With Pope John XXIII: Opening the Windows
to Wisdom, by Alfred McBride, O. Praem.

A Retreat With Thea Bowman and Bede Abram: Leaning
On the Lord, by Joseph A. Brown, S.J.

A Retreat With Teresa of Avila: Living by Holy Wit,
by Gloria Hutchinson

A Retreat With Therese of Lisieux: Loving Our Way Into
Holiness, by Elizabeth Ruth Obbard, O.D.C.

A Retreat With Thomas Merton: Becoming Who We Are,
by Dr. Anthony T. Padovano

A Retreat With Elizabeth Seton

Meeting Our Grace

Judith Metz, S.C.

ST. ANTHONY MESSENGER PRESS

Cincinnati, Ohio

Excerpts from *Elizabeth Seton*, edited by Ellin Kelly and Annabelle Melville, copyright ©1987 by Dr. Ellin M. Kelly and Dr. Annabelle M. Melville, are used by permission of Paulist Press, Inc.

Excerpts from material from the archives of the Sisters of Charity of Mount St. Joseph, Ohio; the Sisters of Charity of St. Elizabeth, Convent Station, N.J.; the Sisters of Charity of Seton Hill, Greensburg, Penn.; and Saint Joseph's Provincial House, Emmitsburg, Md., are reprinted by permission.

Excerpts from *Numerous Choirs, Vol. I* are used by permission of Daughters of Charity of St. Vincent de Paul, Mater Dei Provincialate, 9400 New Harmony Road, Evansville, Ind.

The excerpt from *Gift From the Sea* by Anne Morrow Lindbergh, copyright ©1955, 1975 by Anne Morrow Lindbergh, is reprinted by permission of Pantheon Books, a division of Random House, Inc.

The excerpt from *Let's Pray/2* by Brother Charles Reutemann, F.S.C., is reprinted by permission of the author.

Excerpts from *The Soul of Elizabeth Seton*, by Joseph I. Dirvin, C.M., copyright ©1990 by Ignatius Press, San Francisco, are reprinted with permission of Ignatius Press. All rights reserved.

Scripture quotations are from the *New Revised Standard Version of the Bible*, copyright ©1989, by the Division of Christian Education of the National Council of the Churches of Christ in the USA. Used by permission. All rights reserved.

Cover illustration by Steve Erspamer, S.M.
Cover and book design by Mary Alfieri
Electronic format and pagination by Sandy L. Digman

ISBN 0-86716-304-6

Copyright ©1999, Judith Metz, S.C.

All rights reserved.

Published by St. Anthony Messenger Press
Printed in the U.S.A.

Contents

Introducing A Retreat With...

Twenty years ago I made a weekend retreat at a Franciscan house on the coast of New Hampshire. The retreat director's opening talk was as lively as a long-range weather forecast. He told us how completely God loves each one of us—without benefit of lively anecdotes or fresh insights.

As the friar rambled on, my inner critic kept up a *sotto voce* commentary: "I've heard all this before." "Wish he'd say something new that I could chew on." "That poor man really doesn't have much to say." Ever hungry for manna yet untasted, I devalued any experience of hearing the same old thing.

After a good night's sleep, I awoke feeling as peaceful as a traveler who has at last arrived safely home. I walked across the room toward the closet. On the way I passed the sink with its small framed mirror on the wall above. Something caught my eye like an unexpected presence. I turned, saw the reflection in the mirror and said aloud, "No wonder he loves me!"

This involuntary affirmation stunned me. What or whom had I seen in the mirror? When I looked again, it was "just me," an ordinary person with a lower-than-average reservoir of self-esteem. But I knew that in the initial vision I had seen God-in-me breaking through like a sudden sunrise.

At that moment I knew what it meant to be made in the divine image. I understood right down to my size eleven feet what it meant to be loved exactly as I was.

Only later did I connect this revelation with one granted to the Trappist monk-writer Thomas Merton. As he reports in *Conjectures of a Guilty Bystander*, while standing all unsuspecting on a street corner one day, he was overwhelmed by the "joy of being...a member of a race in which God Himself became incarnate.... There is no way of telling people that they are all walking around shining like the sun."

As an absentminded homemaker may leave a wedding ring on the kitchen windowsill, so I have often mislaid this precious conviction. But I have never forgotten that particular retreat. It persuaded me that the Spirit rushes in where it will. Not even a boring director or a judgmental retreatant can withstand the "violent wind" that "fills the entire house" where we dwell in expectation (see Acts 2:2).

So why deny ourselves any opportunity to come aside awhile and rest on holy ground? Why not withdraw from the daily web that keeps us muddled and wound? Wordsworth's complaint is ours as well: "The world is too much with us." There is no flu shot to protect us from infection by the skepticism of the media, the greed of commerce, the alienating influence of technology. We need retreats as the deer needs the running stream.

An Invitation

This book and its companions in the *A Retreat With...* series from St. Anthony Messenger Press are designed to meet that need. They are an invitation to choose as director some of the most powerful, appealing and wise mentors our faith tradition has to offer.

Our directors come from many countries, historical eras and schools of spirituality. At times they are teamed to sing in close harmony (for example, Francis de Sales, Jane de Chantal and Aelred of Rievaulx on spiritual friendship). Others are paired to kindle an illuminating fire from the friction of their differing views (such as Augustine of Hippo and Mary Magdalene on human sexuality). All have been chosen because, in their humanness and their holiness, they can help us grow in self-knowledge, discernment of God's will and maturity in the Spirit.

Inviting us into relationship with these saints and holy ones are inspired authors from today's world, women and men whose creative gifts open our windows to the Spirit's flow. As a motto for the authors of our series, we have borrowed the advice of Dom Frederick Dunne to the young Thomas Merton. Upon joining the Trappist monks, Merton wanted to sacrifice his writing activities lest they interfere with his contemplative vocation. Dom Frederick wisely advised, "Keep on writing books that make people love the spiritual life."

That is our motto. Our purpose is to foster (or strengthen) friendships between readers and retreat directors—friendships that feed the soul with wisdom, past and present. Like the scribe "trained for the kingdom of heaven," each author brings forth from his or her storeroom "what is new and what is old" (Matthew 13:52).

The Format

The pattern for each *A Retreat With...* remains the same; readers of one will be in familiar territory when they move on to the next. Each book is organized as a seven-session retreat that readers may adapt to their own schedules or to the needs of a group.

Day One begins with an anecdotal introduction called "Getting to Know Our Directors." Readers are given a telling glimpse of the guides with whom they will be sharing the retreat experience. A second section, "Placing Our Directors in Context," will enable retreatants to see the guides in their own historical, geographical, cultural and spiritual settings.

Having made the human link between seeker and guide, the authors go on to "Introducing Our Retreat Theme." This section clarifies how the guide(s) are especially suited to explore the theme and how the retreatant's spirituality can be nourished by it.

After an original "Opening Prayer" to breathe life into the day's reflection, the author, speaking with and through the mentor(s), will begin to spin out the theme. While focusing on the guide(s)' own words and experience, the author may also draw on Scripture, tradition, literature, art, music, psychology or contemporary events to illuminate the path.

Each day's session is followed by reflection questions designed to challenge, affirm and guide the reader in integrating the theme into daily life. A "Closing Prayer" brings the session full circle and provides a spark of inspiration for the reader to harbor until the next session.

Days Two through Six begin with "Coming Together in the Spirit" and follow a format similar to Day One. Day Seven weaves the entire retreat together, encourages a continuation of the mentoring relationship and concludes with "Deepening Your Acquaintance," an envoi to live the theme by God's grace, the director(s)' guidance and the retreatant's discernment. A closing section of Resources serves as a larder from which readers may draw enriching books, videos, cassettes and films.

We hope readers will experience at least one of those memorable "No wonder God loves me!" moments. And we hope that they will have "talked back" to the mentors, as good friends are wont to do.

A case in point: There was once a famous preacher who always drew a capacity crowd to the cathedral. Whenever he spoke, an eccentric old woman sat in the front pew directly beneath the pulpit. She took every opportunity to mumble complaints and contradictions— just loud enough for the preacher to catch the drift that he was not as wonderful as he was reputed to be. Others seated down front glowered at the woman and tried to shush her. But she went right on needling the preacher to her heart's content.

When the old woman died, the congregation was astounded at the depth and sincerity of the preacher's grief. Asked why he was so bereft, he responded, "Now who will help me to grow?"

All of our mentors in *A Retreat With...* are worthy guides. Yet none would seek retreatants who simply said, "Where you lead, I will follow. You're the expert." In truth, our directors provide only half the retreat's content. Readers themselves will generate the other half.

As general editor for the retreat series, I pray that readers will, by their questions, comments, doubts and decision-making, fertilize the seeds our mentors have planted.

And may the Spirit of God rush in to give the growth.

Gloria Hutchinson
Series Editor
Conversion of Saint Paul, 1995

Getting to Know Our Director

Introducing Elizabeth Seton

There is often a warm glow of light in the tiny paned window. The small, frail woman wrapped in a black shawl is writing letters by the light of a single candle long after the students and other sisters in the house have retired. This dedication to her family, friends, sisters and former students demands a commitment of time that is not available other than late at night. "Take care of yourself, you need your rest," the sisters urge her. But she cares so deeply. To her, it is worth the sacrifice to nurture these relationships.

One of Elizabeth Seton's early companions in founding the Sisters of Charity is leaving in the morning for the orphanage in New York. The foundress knows she will keenly miss her, but Margaret's talents are needed...and so Elizabeth pens a farewell note expressing her deep love and concern for each sister:

My Margaret—His peace
Beg Rose to do all she can to get Fanny home...to let Cecil have all the time she can with her parents as she passes. [T]ake care of Margaret exactly as you would of E.A.S. Mind that, my last injunction.... Watch carefully to make Felicite happy and the health of Scholastica who cannot bear much wet and cold, you know. I am not uneasy about her happiness or yours. You have so much to do for our Lord. May he bless you as my heart and soul bless you![1]

Whether as a devoted friend or family member, as a wife enduring the wrenching experience of her husband's slow death on foreign soil, or as a religious superior encouraging and directing her sisters, Elizabeth's letters and journals were an extension of her loving friendships. She poured herself out for others and invited them to do so in return. She cultivated the deep relationships which were a mainstay in her life. Though she longed for quiet and solitude, that was not the path God had chosen for her. She always seemed to be surrounded by children, responsibilities and demands on her time. The path of her life was to be traveled with others.

Born in New York on August 28, 1774, Elizabeth Bayley was a child of the American Revolution. Coming from a prominent and respected family, she could look forward to the comforts and advantages of the gentry. Yet, from an early age her life was one of contrasts: between privilege and hardship, between intense joy and profound suffering. But it was also a life lived in God's presence from its earliest days. Death was an early visitor in her life—her mother died when Elizabeth was just three, and her younger sister died the following year. Perhaps these experiences caused her to turn so readily to God as a loving parent. Her sense of God's sustaining love stayed with her throughout her life.

Elizabeth's widowed father quickly remarried but his new home was not a welcoming place for Elizabeth and her older sister, Mary. The two spent their childhood years shuttling between New York City and their uncle's home. It was there, in New Rochelle, that the young girl cultivated a delight in nature and enjoyed spending time alone by the water of Long Island Sound. She experienced a sacredness in nature and fostered a deep connection with its bounty and beauty.

As she neared twenty, Elizabeth was caught up in the

social world of theater, dances and parties. She met and married William Magee Seton, heir to a prominent shipping business. Their home was a happy one and their early years together were prosperous and blessed with children. Their firstborn, Anna Maria (Annina), arrived in May 1795—just sixteen months into their married life. She was quickly followed by her brothers, William and Richard. Catherine (Kit) and Rebecca were born in 1800 and 1802, respectively.

Even before the younger children were born, however, economic difficulties and William's declining health cast ponderous shadows over the family. Through these trials Elizabeth's intimate relationship with God deepened and she formed several important and lasting friendships. As she matured, the intensity of her devotion to God and enthusiasm for sharing that devotion with others grew. This became a sustaining force for the remainder of her life. To one friend she commented:

The nearer a soul is truly united to God the more its sensibilities are increased to every being of His creation; much more to those whom it is bound to love by the tenderest and most endearing ties.[2]

Elizabeth became a prolific writer in her adult life. She is at her best when pouring out poignant reflections on the events of her own life and identifying these with the life of Jesus. Her intense emotion carries readers into the pain or ecstasy of her experiences. She is able to share a wisdom gained from living prayerfully and incorporating a profound faith that God is present and acting through the everyday circumstances of life. She urges, admonishes and challenges her confidants to enter more deeply into their relationship with God. This sharing seemed to sustain her—to help her discover her own deepest identity as well as to nurture others to greater heights.

In an attempt to rejuvenate William's health, they traveled by sea to Italy—the effort was fruitless. William died in December, 1803, but the trip proved providential. During her four months there, Elizabeth was deeply impressed by the generosity and the devout Catholicism of her hosts, the Filicchi family. In addition, her religious sensitivities led her to be moved by the magnificent churches and solemn rituals of Catholicism. The young widow felt drawn to this religion, though it was reviled in her homeland.

After her return, Elizabeth experienced a wrenching nine months before she made her commitment to the Catholic Church. As well she knew, this decision would drive a wedge between her and many of her family members and friends. Thus, she lost the support that should have sustained her as a widow and single parent struggling to maintain her family.

After three years of rejection and financial hardship, Elizabeth experienced a brighter horizon. At the invitation of the Sulpician priests and Bishop John Carroll, she moved her family to Baltimore to open a school. To her surprise, she soon found herself the center of a nascent community of women interested in living religious life in the United States. Elizabeth fit the role of "Mother" well. She was warm and nurturing, self-sacrificing, strong and courageous, challenging and encouraging. She offered an unconditional love to each sister in her uniqueness.

Donated property outside the rural Maryland village of Emmitsburg became the motherhouse of the American Sisters of Charity. Elizabeth spent her last years there among her sisters and students. She shared life fully with them as they prayed, studied and enjoyed the beauty of their valley home. She especially looked forward to their Sunday treks to the local parish church at Mount St.

Mary's where she taught catechism to the local children and spent the afternoon in quiet prayer on the wooded hillside near Our Lady's grotto.

In her years at Emmitsburg, Elizabeth experienced a series of heart-wrenching losses through death: two young sisters-in-law who were like daughters to her, two of her own daughters and several of her religious companions. As deep as these relationships were, though, the death of loved ones never prevented her from loving again with passion and intensity. She continued to send off and welcome sisters and students. We can imagine her tear-filled goodbyes and exuberant receptions continuing until she succumbed to the "family complaint" of tuberculosis on January 4, 1821.

In her full life of forty-five years, Elizabeth Seton had become a woman for all seasons: wife, mother, widow, single parent, convert, educator, friend, mentor, religious foundress. She was a person deeply in love with God and with others. She found her God in the everyday, in every moment, and lived these days and moments as the beginning of her eternity. Goethe could well have been referring to her when he wrote:

> At each moment she starts upon a long journey
> and at each moment reaches her end...
> All is eternally present in her
> for she knows neither past or future.
> For her the present is eternity.[3]

Placing Our Director in Context

Elizabeth Seton's World

"Elizabeth Ann Seton was wholly american. She had the blood of French, English and Dutch Colonial pioneers in her veins." She was of "'rooted American stock'; both of her parents and two of her grandparents were born here. When our great Republic was born, she became a charter American citizen."[4]

Born in New York during the tumultuous times leading to the formal Declaration of Independence of the thirteen British colonies from their mother country, Elizabeth Seton participated in the birthing of the American nation. Her home city was occupied by the British army during the Revolutionary War and withdrew only in 1783 when Elizabeth was nine years old. Her teenage years were spent as the former colonies were struggling to overcome rivalries to form themselves into a new nation, culminating in the adoption of the Constitution in 1789.

Intellectually this period was shaped by Enlightenment thought. Isaac Newton's discovery of "natural laws" which governed the physical world set off an explosion of new thought and theory. Intellectuals developed a tremendous confidence in the power of human reason and eventually came to redefine God, the world and themselves. The English philosopher John Locke extended Newton's natural law approach to the interaction of people in society, defining natural laws as life, liberty and property. These doctrines penetrated society widely. Clubs were formed to discuss them, and as they were disseminated, they were enthusiastically embraced. The influence of French philosophers such as Voltaire and Rousseau was felt on the French Revolution, but these thinkers also had a wide readership in the United States. For some the Enlightenment ideas were hostile to religion, for others they were the cause of indifference. It is estimated that in the 1790's only ten percent of the American people attended Sunday church services. Elizabeth herself was caught up in the currents of the times. She embraced Rousseau's writings and, in one note to a friend, she remarked, *"Dear J.J. [Jean Jacques] I am yours!"*[5] and noted in one of her journals: *"My Merciful Saviour, I too have felt their fatal Influence and once they composed my* Sunday *devotion."*[6]

Deism, with its belief in a mechanistic God, was the popular religious expression of the day. In 1805, when Elizabeth was involved in a project to start a school in New York, she met resistance because of her Catholicism. Her friends told her they "did not fear a Deist teacher but a Roman Catholic is thought of with horror."[7]

Elizabeth Seton was born into a well-to-do environment and afforded the advantages of her class. She enjoyed the benefits of a good education, summers in the country and an active social life. But she was also deeply influenced by her prominent physician-father Richard Bayley who took a leading role in the fight to combat disease and the conditions that fostered it. In 1797 he accepted the position of public health officer of the New York Board of Health Commissioners and, when sick immigrants were detained on Staten Island, he assumed the duties of quarantine officer. It was here he died in 1801, caring for victims of the yellow fever epidemic being carried by ships arriving in New York Harbor.

Elizabeth herself was no stranger to benevolent activity. She was an active member and officer in the Society for the Relief of Poor Widows with Small Children, the first benevolent society managed by women in the United States. Even as she was raising her own young family in the late 1790's, she devoted much time and energy to visiting the poor, bringing them what relief she could.

New York, a major port, was in the midst of the economic activity of the growing nation. Second only to Philadelphia in size, it was a cosmopolitan city with hundreds of merchant vessels annually making calls to deposit and load wares. In 1794, Elizabeth married William Seton, a member of one of the city's prominent merchant families. After the death of her father-in-law who was a principal in Seton, Maitland and Company, Elizabeth assisted her husband in the running of the business. The business was finally brought to bankruptcy in 1800, partially because of French and British attacks on American shipping in blatant disregard of declared American neutrality in the Napoleonic Wars.

Elizabeth was a true daughter of America in her Protestant roots. She was accustomed to religious pluralism, freedom of religion, and separation of church and state. Raised a member of the Episcopal church, she loved the Scriptures and incorporated phrases and allusions to them in her own writing. She entered a new phase of religious devotion under the influence of Reverend John Henry Hobart, who became assistant at Trinity Church in 1800. Hobart was a man of great zeal and moving oratory, someone on the cutting edge of the Second Great Awakening in American religious history.

Elizabeth's Protestant roots also led her to expect the clergy to offer spiritual direction and counseling, and she continued to look to them for guidance after her conversion to Catholicism. In addition, her appreciation of the importance of the sermon to the Sunday worship service was influenced by her early experiences. She frequently commented on the content and delivery of sermons in her notes and letters, and she did not hesitate to admonish priest-friends who did not make proper preparations for their preaching responsibilities.

One of the central components of Elizabeth's spirituality was her devotion to the Eucharist. In the Episcopal church of her time the communion service was celebrated about six times a year and most believers

accepted a spiritual but not an objective presence of
Christ in the Eucharist. Even so, this service was a focal
point of Elizabeth Seton's prayer life. At times when she
was unable to attend the communion service, she would
emulate its elements at home in prayer. When she was
introduced to the Catholic belief in the real presence of
Christ in the Eucharist, she was immediately caught up in
it, writing to her beloved sister-in-law, Rebecca, "*My sister
dear, How happy we would be if we believed what these poor
souls believe, that they* possess God *in the Sacrament and that
he remains in their churches and is carried to them when they
are sick...*"[8]

Essentially it was this difference in doctrine which
most influenced her decision to enter the Catholic Church,
and she joyously celebrated her own First Communion as
a Catholic, writing to Amabilia Filicchi in Italy, "*I count
the days and hours—yet a few more of hope and expectation....
At last Amabilia—at last—GOD IS MINE and I AM HIS—
now let all go its round—I HAVE RECEIVED HIM.*"[9]

The Church she joined in 1805 was emerging from the
experience of being a tiny persecuted minority in the
United States. The Catholic congregation in New York
had been meeting publicly for less than twenty years and
for the most part was comprised of poor Irish immigrants
who were regarded as the "offscourings of the people"
and "a public Nuisance."[10] This reality, however, did not
deter the ardent convert who felt she had found the true
faith.

Fortunately, she was soon put in touch with educated
and cultured members of the Church, both clergy and lay.
The most influential of these was Bishop John Carroll,
whose impact on the formation of the Church in the
United States is inestimable. A true product of the
Enlightenment, Carroll supported the ideals of the
American society and saw no conflict between them and

Catholic values. He worked to make Catholicism intelligible to the American society and that society intelligible to Church hierarchy in Rome. He often praised the religious climate of the new nation and saw conditions here as the best hope for the future of Catholicism.

It was Carroll and the Reverend William DuBourg, S.S., who were instrumental in encouraging Elizabeth Seton to move to Baltimore and start life anew after her conversion. Both were interested in promoting education for women and saw Elizabeth as the focal point for this effort. Besides the establishment of a school, however, her move also led to the founding of the Sisters of Charity, the first apostolic community of women religious in the United States. With the beginnings of the community came the necessity of adopting a Rule. Using that of the French Daughters of Charity as a model, changes were made, appropriate to their American circumstances.

Importantly, their rule recognized the need for flexibility, allowing for modifications in habit, customs and manners according to local differences. But the spirit of the rule was true to Saint Vincent de Paul's original. Charity was the principal aim of the institute. The sisters were to cherish and respect one another, and their spiritual exercises, while important, were not to prevent them from being available to people in need.

Elizabeth herself affirmed that she never had a thought discordant with these rules, and in exuberance described to her friend Julia Scott, *"the joy of my soul at the prospect of being able to assist the poor, visit the sick, comfort the sorrowful, clothe little innocents and teach them to love God!"*[11]

A retreat with Elizabeth Seton is an opportunity to be drawn into a deeper and more wholehearted love of God experienced in relationships and in the busyness of everyday life—but always in the light of eternity.

Notes

[1] Elizabeth Seton to Sister Margaret George, Emmitsburg, 28 May 1819, Archives, Mount St. Joseph, Ohio.

[2] Joseph B. Code, *Letters of Mother Seton to Mrs. Julianna Scott* (New York: The Father Salvator M. Burgio Memorial Foundation in Honor of Mother Seton, 1960), p. 188.

[3] From the poem "Lauds," quoted in *The Soul of the World* (New York: HarperCollins, 1993).

[4] Francis Cardinal Spellman's foreword to Joseph I. Dirvin, C.M., *Mrs. Seton: Foundress of the American Sisters of Charity* (New York: Farrar, Straus and Cudahy, Inc., 1962), p. ix.

[5] Annabelle Melville, *Elizabeth Bayley Seton* (St. Paul, Minn.: Carillon Books, 1976), p. 64.

[6] Ellin Kelly and Annabelle Melville, eds., *Elizabeth Seton: Selected Writings* (New York: Paulist Press, 1987), p. 224.

[7] Kelly and Melville, p. 183.

[8] Kelly and Melville, p. 133.

[9] Kelly and Melville, pp. 166, 167.

[10] Kelly and Melville, pp. 163-164.

[11] Code, p. 182.

DAY ONE

For Better or for Worse

Introducing Our Retreat Theme

"This isn't the pace at which we want to be living—dinner at 7:30, working on weekends to catch up," a friend recently remarked. Most of us feel caught up in the demands of the everyday. We make innumerable resolutions that we will not allow our daily lives to spin out of control while we try to respond to the multiple demands placed on us. And yet, busyness steals our focus. We rush from one thing to another without making the mental and psychological, much less spiritual, adjustments necessary to be present to what we are about. We are short with people because we are short on time. We end our day exhausted and short-tempered instead of nourished and fulfilled. And we ask ourselves, "How can we escape this crush?"

There are many gurus in our world offering us assistance in gaining physical, mental and psychological wholeness. We spend millions of dollars each year in efforts to achieve more satisfying and healthy lives. Our retreat director offers no quick fixes, miracles or magic solutions to our human condition. Instead, she simply encourages us to *"keep well to what you believe to be the grace of the moment...only do your best and leave the rest to our dear God."*[1]

Because her life was filled with many people and

constant demands, Elizabeth Seton can offer an
abundance of wisdom gained from the practicalities of
everyday experience. Living the mystery of God in the
present moment grew in her as a result of living
prayerfully and reflectively. As she matured, she became
ever more watchful with eager longing for the intrusions
of grace in whatever form they might appear. She saw all
as coming from the hand of her beloved God, and it was
her passion for the present moment that grounded
Elizabeth in eternity. She is as delighted to share her
insights with us as she was to share them with her dearest
friends and her religious daughters. As she observed, "*We
must be so careful to meet our grace—wherever we go 'there is
a store of grace waiting....'*"[2]

Opening Prayer

Loving God, you chose us, chose us in Christ to live
in your presence through love. We praise you for having
given us your grace and for your desire to bring
everything together under Christ. Grant us the wisdom to
understand the mystery of bringing all in heaven and on
earth together in Christ. We pray that Christ may live in
our hearts through faith. We pray that, with all the saints,
we will have the strength to grasp the breadth and the
length, the height and the depth; we pray that, knowing
the love of Christ, which is beyond all knowledge, we
will be filled with the utter fullness of God (adapted from
Ephesians 1:3-10, 3:16-19).

Retreat Session One

"I'm so delighted you came in the spring, it's our loveliest time of year," exudes the small woman with the dark, sparkling eyes. She is waiting for us, under the large oak tree near the cemetery. Her broad, welcoming smile and warm demeanor embrace each of us and immediately create a relaxed atmosphere and a bond among the retreatants.

"Our home in St. Joseph's Valley is spectacular now," she goes on. "I want you to immerse yourself in the beauty of the countryside and feel the assurance of God's abiding love during these days of retreat. Look around you! The rhododendrons always excite me when they bloom, and I never cease to be thrilled when the trees are in their spring newness. And notice how many shades of green there are!" she encourages us.

We are immediately caught up in the enthusiasm of the speaker. Her love of people is apparent, and the comments we have heard about how she thrives on sharing deeply already seem borne out. Well-spoken and articulate, our director expresses herself easily in poetic and scriptural language. She carries herself as someone with a proper upbringing and a good education. Even in her simple black dress and cap, her appearance is impressive.

"I've been enjoying the utter peacefulness of the morning," Elizabeth comments. "The movement of the air, the gentle warmth of the sun and the sounds of nature always lead me into an appreciation of God's enduring love. I often find myself recalling past experiences of becoming engrossed in nature and from there I am drawn into God's presence in a particularly moving way."

She pauses, collects herself and exclaims, "*God is my*

guide *my* friend *and* Supporter—*With such a guide can I fear, with such a friend shall I not be* satisfied, *with such a supporter can I fall?"*[3]

Elizabeth begins by sharing with us her firm conviction that God's affectionate and steadfast love for us is the model for all our relationships. She reminds us of God's promise:

Can a woman forget her nursing child,
or show no compassion for the child of her womb?
Even these may forget,
yet I will not forget you (Isaiah 49:15).

She talks about the characteristics of God's faithful love. First is a willingness to demonstrate our affection. As God unceasingly pours love upon us in many visible ways, so we are called to reciprocate in our relationships both with God and with those we love. Second is unswerving loyalty regardless of whether it is returned. Despite all the vagrancies of Israel's relationship with God, they remained the chosen people. And Jesus himself promised that he would not leave us orphans. Lastly, this saintly woman reminds us, is the living out of relationships in selfless action. Jesus modeled such action on the cross pouring out the very substance of himself despite the cost. So we are to imitate his action. There is no greater love than to lay down one's life for one's friends!

The first ardent love of Elizabeth's life was her husband, William, and as she opens her hand she proudly reveals a framed miniature painting of him. Deep love radiating from her face, she indicates it should be passed among us.

The two married in 1894 before Elizabeth was twenty years old. Their relationship was joyful and fulfilling for both. They shared many interests, particularly music: William had the Stradivarius he had purchased in Europe; she her treasured piano. The sounds of their duets often filled their home. They cherished each other and often exchanged notes when apart. On one such occasion he found a picture of her tucked in his shaving case. She considered him *"my friend," "my dearest treasure."* He, in turn, regarded her as his *"old knot of oak."*[4] And when he came from the city on one of his frequent visits to their summer cottage she exuded, *"Could it be imagined that All the scene changes when he is here—Countenances, everything wears the smile, and really this has been as happy a day to me as a mortal ought to have."*[5]

The deep affection between the couple continued through their nearly ten years of marriage. Proud and devoted parents of five children, Elizabeth and William thrilled at spending time with their offspring. The one qualifying factor was William's lack of interest in religion while Elizabeth's interest was advancing significantly. After encouraging her husband in his prayer life for years, she at last saw God break through. *"The last twenty-four hours [have] been the happiest I have ever seen or could expect, as the most earnest wish of my heart [is] fulfilled,"* she exclaimed. *"Willy's heart seemed to be nearer to me for being nearer to his God."*[6] From this point on they were able to share on a level they had never before experienced.

Elizabeth understood that her love for her husband was a covenant relationship meant to endure through all the vicissitudes of life, faithful as God's love of the Israelite people. Although their first years together had been happy and prosperous, by 1799 they faced both bankruptcy and the toll of William's increasingly debilitating tuberculosis. He was frantic with worry because of their financial situation and his moods ranged between apathy and despair. *"You know Willy's disposition,"* she wrote to Rebecca, *"sometimes he says he will work it out, at others Nothing but State Prison and poverty. For one intire [sic] week we wrote till one or two in the morning and he never closed his eyes till daylight and then for not more than an hour."*[7]

Even though his wife shed bitter tears over the loss of their home, she continued to believe that where hope and love existed, nothing was irreparable. She faced the future with serenity, placing her reliance on God's faithful love. Written reflections offer insight into her trust.

Elizabeth saw the inner peace she was experiencing amidst their troubles as a gift of God's love and a sign of God's continuing affection.

To be assured of that love is enough to tie us faithfully to him and while we have fidelity to him all the surrounding cares and contradictions of this Life are but Cords of mercy to send us faster to Him....[8]

The cup that our Father has given us, shall we not drink it? "Blessed Saviour! by the bitterness of thy pains we may estimate the force of thy love..., thou wouldst not willingly call on us to suffer, thou hast declared unto us that all things shall work together for our Good if we are faithful to thee, and therefore if thou so ordainest it, welcome disappointment and Poverty, welcome sickness and pain—welcome even shame and contempt, and calumny. If this be a rough and thorny path it is one which thou hast gone before us...meanwhile thou wilt support us with the consolations of thy Grace...."[9]

A trip to Italy in an effort to restore William's health filled Elizabeth with homesickness and longing for her children. Her journal entries fluctuate between misery and exalted faith. *"If I could forget my God one moment at these times I should go mad—but He hushes all—Be still and know that I am God your Father,"*[10] she writes.

Elizabeth manifested a selfless love in her unswerving devotion to her husband, particularly during their month-long sojourn in an Italian *lazaretto* where they were medically quarantined upon their arrival. Bolted and barred like prisoners in this dungeon-like structure, they resided in a cold, dank cell with a brick floor and bare walls. The beleaguered woman cared for her dying husband physically and spiritually with hardly a thought to her own needs or comfort, frequently reflecting on Jesus' total sacrifice on the cross. The single window, double grated with iron, admitted wind that almost extinguished their light and blew on her William until he shivered with the cold. His melancholy face, wasting physical condition, racking cough and despairing sobs strained her emotionally. She prayed with him, *"giving words to his soul which was too weak to pray for itself."*[11]

During his final illness, Elizabeth was her husband's greatest source of inspiration. They spent their time together crying, praying and reading Scripture until fatigue overcame them. She experienced an "agony of sorrow" with her eyes smarting so much from crying, wind and fatigue that she had to close them and lift up her heart to God. And yet, she called these *"days of grace"* for William's thoughts turned almost constantly toward heaven, and he experienced a serene resignation.[12]

In his last agony he refused to have anyone but his wife present. *"But,"* she recalled, *"to see that character exalted to the Peaceful Humble Christian, waiting the will of God with a Patience that seems more than human, and a firm faith which would do honor to the most distinguished Piety, is a happiness allowed only to the poor little Mother who is separated from all other happiness that is connected with this scene of things."*[13]

And she confided to her sister-in-law, *"I have been to my dear Seton's grave—and wept plentifully over it with the unrestrained affection which the last sufferings of his life, added to remembrance of former years, had made almost more than precious—when you read my daily memorandums...you will feel what my love has been, and acknowledge that God alone could support...such proofs as have been required of it."*[14]

"In all this it is not necessary to dwell on the mercy and consoling presence of my dear Redeemer, for no mortal strength could support what I experienced."[15]

Left a widow with five young children, she cried abundantly at the full loneliness and sadness of her case, and confided, *"my poor high heart was in the clouds roving after my William's soul and repeating my God you are my God, and so I am now alone in the world with you and my little ones but you are my Father and doubly theirs."*[16]

By this time the miniature has made its way back to Elizabeth's hand. She gazes at it fondly and then looks off into the distance as if remembering the joys rather than the sorrows of her married life. No matter how difficult, how trying, they were days spent in faithful love—love mirroring God's steadfastness.

"And now," she says, "I leave you to your own reminiscences of how God has been faithful to you and how you have mirrored this faithfulness in your relationships with others."

For Reflection

- *Recall an instance in your life when you were able to let go into God's boundless mercy. What were the effects of this experience on you?*

- *Imagine or draw a picture of how "the cares and contradictions of life are but Cords of mercy to send us faster to Him...."*

- *Recall in your own experience someone who gave care to another so that it seemed as if "God alone could support such proofs as were required" of that person. Reflect on what the meaning of this was for you.*

- *Elizabeth showed her deep devotion and loyalty to her*

husband in circumstances of sickness and financial reverses. What circumstances might challenge your loyalty to your spouse or friends? How might you respond?

Closing Prayer

Choose one or more of these paired passages from the word of God and the work of Elizabeth Seton. Read, reread and pray with these words of faithfulness. Invite God to bless you with a sense of being unconditionally loved.

From the word of God:

"I have made a covenant with my chosen one,
I have sworn to my servant David:
'I will establish your descendants forever,
and build your throne for all generations.'"
(Psalm 89:3-4).

From the work of Elizabeth: *Glory Glory Glory [be] to Him who has obtained for his servant these inestimable privileges— to enter into covenant with him—to commune with his spirit— to receive the blessing of our reconciled Father—Inheritors in his Kingdom of Blessedness.*[17]

From the word of God:

But now thus says the Lord,...
Do not fear, for I have redeemed you;
I have called you by name, you are mine.
When you pass through the waters, I will be with you;
and through the rivers, they shall not overwhelm you;
when you walk through fire, you shall not be burned,
and the flame shall not consume you.
For I am the Lord, your God,
the Holy One of Israel, your Savior (Isaiah 43:1-3).

From the work of Elizabeth: *Only to reflect—If we did not* now *know and love God—If we did not* feel *the consolations, and* embrace *the chearing [sic] Hope he has set before us, and* find *our* delight *in the study of his blessed word and Truth* What *would become of us?*[18]

Notes

[1] Charles I. White, *Mother Seton, Mother of Many Daughters* (Garden City, N.Y.: Doubleday, 1949), p. 258.

[2] Kelly and Melville, p. 303.

[3] Kelly and Melville, p. 89.

[4] Code, p. 86.

[5] Elizabeth Seton to Rebecca Seton, Summer, 1801, Archives of the Sisters of Charity of Saint Elizabeth, Convent Station, N. J., #139-142.

[6] Melville, p. 95.

[7] Elizabeth Seton to Rebecca Seton, 3 January 1800, Archives Convent Station, #464-467.

[8] Kelly and Melville, p. 84.

[9] Kelly and Melville, p. 84.

[10] Kelly and Melville, p. 109.

[11] Kelly and Melville, p. 108.

[12] Melville, p. 103.

[13] Kelly and Melville, p. 119.

[14] Kelly and Melville, p. 100.

[15] Kelly and Melville, p. 125.

[16] Kelly and Melville, p. 130.

[17] Kelly and Melville, p. 88.

[18] Kelly and Melville, p. 111.

Day Two
'A Cloud Before My Path'

Coming Together in the Spirit

Several years ago I signed up for a night hike at a nature preserve in Massachusetts. To my surprise, as the group started down the dark path, our leader instructed us, "No flashlights! Your eyes will adjust."

Initially hesitant and fearful of stumbling, I picked my way along the rocky and root-embedded hillsides. But, trusting in the guide's wisdom, I moved through the darkness. Almost imperceptibly a transition began to occur. What had formerly seemed shrouded and indistinct began to emerge and seem clearly lit by the moon. My "night vision" had kicked in. The familiarity and peace of walking among the wonders of God's creation returned with a new sense of discovery at experiencing it as never before. I knew that my guide's instruction had been worthy of my trust and had opened new wonders of beauty and insight to me.

Defining Our Thematic Context

On Day One we were reminded that God is our faithful guide, friend and supporter. Elizabeth helped us to realize the connection between God's promise of a covenant relationship and our call to live our commitments to others in fidelity. Our mentor's happy and fulfilling days with her husband were always lived in the consciousness of God's overarching faithfulness to her. As in most of our relationships, there is a "for better" and a "for worse." She showed us ways to "meet our grace" in both. Suggesting that the central element is always "being drawn nearer to God by being drawn near to others," she encouraged us to ponder how this goal might come closer to reality in our own lives.

Today she leads us into another scenario we have all experienced: struggling for light as we go through a difficult decision-making process. Sometimes it seems that the harder we struggle the more deeply we feel ourselves mired in darkness. We shout to God to free us from this ensnarement. We pray and beg for insight and inspiration, but still it seems there is a "cloud before our path." Perhaps we are being asked to blindly trust until our "night vision" takes over.

Opening Prayer

My Lord God,
I have no idea where I am going.
I do not see the road ahead of me.
I cannot know for certain where it will end.
Nor do I really know myself, and the fact that I think I
am following your will does not mean that I am
actually doing so.
But I believe that desire to please you does in fact
please you.
And I hope I have that desire in all that I am doing.
I hope that I will never do anything apart from that
desire.
And I know that if I do this you will lead me by the
right

road though I may know nothing about it.
Therefore will I trust you always though I may seem
    to be
lost and in the shadow of death.
I will not fear, for you are ever with me, and you will
    never
leave me to face my perils alone.[1]

Retreat Session Two

Once again we are blessed with a sunny day and
Elizabeth seems as sparkling as the creek. Our director
has instructed us to meet her at Tom's Creek, a short walk
from the buildings on community property at
Emmitsburg. The stream bordered by stately trees
provides a cathedral-like setting. Its seclusion offers a
peacefulness and privacy which invites our spirits into
reflection. Clearly relishing this opportunity to enjoy the
gift of water, this sprightly woman stoops to cradle some
in her hand and thoughtfully lets it run through her
fingers.

"Water makes me think of the most difficult decisions
I ever experienced in my life," she observes. "Yesterday I
told you something of my trip across the Atlantic to Italy.
Today I will share another aspect of it, for it set me on a
voyage that affected the rest of my life!"

"Be still, and know that I am God!"(Psalm 46:10) she
prays in a hushed tone. "God is present during
tumultuous storms and in times when our outlook is
obscured by fog and darkness. As excruciating as it may
be, our task is to patiently wait, always believing that
when the time is right, the clouds will lift and our way

will be clear."

"Recall a time in your life," she gently invites, "when you were faced with a choice that was to have a profound effect on your future." During the silence that follows, only the muted sounds of the creek, the breeze through the trees, and the chirping birds fill the space. Elizabeth herself gazes into the water as if seeing a reflection of times past, a time when she felt like a ship *"drifting on the Ocean without any perceptible approach to its haven of rest."*[2]

When Elizabeth departed on her voyage to Italy she was a committed member of Trinity Episcopal Church and a great admirer of the assistant rector, Reverend John Henry Hobart. His evangelical fervor and oratorical skills fueled the devotion of Elizabeth as well as of other parish members. The two formed a close friendship, with Elizabeth describing him as having her *"unbounded veneration, affection, esteem and the tribute of the 'Heart Sincere.'"*[3]

During her sojourn in Italy, however, Elizabeth was exposed to religion as she had never before experienced it. Always keenly interested in things of the spirit, the young widow was wide-eyed at the grandeur of the churches she visited. These houses of worship reminded her of Biblical accounts of the riches of nature and art which David and Solomon had devoted to the Holy Temple.[4] The hushed light, the ceremony of the Mass and the majestic organ music transported her to a place unfamiliar to one used to a more austere Protestant setting. She was also affected by the devotion of large numbers of kneeling worshipers, so engrossed in their prayer that they were inattentive to anything else.

But most importantly, she was impressed by her hosts. Friends of her husband, the Filicchi family embraced Elizabeth as one of their own during the time of William's last illness and death. They offered her every comfort and consolation possible, taking her and her young daughter, Annina, into their home for the months they were delayed in Italy after William's death. In addition to the care and attention they offered, Elizabeth noted their deep religiosity. She was in awe of their regular schedule of prayers, attendance at Mass and Lenten practices.

Although this American Protestant found aspects of their religion "strange," she opened herself to its beliefs and practices. In fact, she found herself astonished that she was even moved to explore what were foreign doctrines to her. Philip Filicchi was blunt and exhorting as he encouraged her to consider the truths and claims of his religion while his younger brother, Antonio, was more gentle and patient. At times she tried to dismiss the whole thing lightly but frequently found herself on her knees begging God for light to see the path along which she was being called. As soon as her first attendance at Mass she found her beliefs challenged, *"I don't know how to say the awful effect at being where they told me God was present in the blessed sacrament,"* she wrote. And, by the end of her stay in Italy she was clearly inclining toward the Catholic religion. *"Did I not beg [God] to give me their Faith and promise All in return for such a gift[?],"* she wrote in her journal.[5]

A period of interior darkness and struggle that was to last for nearly ten months began for Elizabeth during her fifty-six-day sea voyage home. She had been led into the unknown and this made her fearful and uncertain. Accompanied by Antonio Filicchi on her return trip, she received instruction from him on the tenets of the Catholic faith, and yet she agonized on how it was *"...to be brought to the light of the truth notwithstanding every affection of my heart and power of my will was opposed to it."*[6] Upon her arrival in New York she was caught in the crossfire between her Italian friends and those to whom she was returning. A sense of inner turmoil and indecision dominated Elizabeth's life as she struggled to discern God's will in her search for truth. She found herself vulnerable not only because of her new religious inclinations, but because of her economic and social situation, which forced her to rely for support on others who considered Catholics inferior and unacceptable company.

The one person with whom Elizabeth expected to share her journey during her decision-making process was her sister-in-law, Rebecca. Instead, she found this "soul's sister" on death's door, only waiting for Elizabeth to accompany her in her last days. Stealing what time remained, Elizabeth noted:

A thousand pages could not tell the sweet hours now with my departing Rebecca—the wonder at the few lines I could point out...of the true faith and service to our God—she could only repeat 'Your people are my people, Your God my God,' and every day the delight to see her eagerness to read our Spiritual Mass together until the Sunday morning of our last te deum....[7]

Elizabeth's comfort of sharing with Rebecca was but a brief respite before her struggle erupted with full ferocity. Each side, vying for her soul, gave her books to study to convince her of the validity of their positions. Reverend Hobart described the corruption of Catholics and warned her not to be misled into the church of the anti-Christ. And, in one instance during a visit he became *"so entirely out of all patience...his visit was short and painful on both sides—God direct me for I see it is in vain to look for help from any but him."*[8] At the same time Philip Filicchi admonished her to "stop haggling over details and answer the question: what is the true church established by Christ?"[9]

Elizabeth found herself off balance as she tried to hear God in a new way. Eventually she realized her search for truth had to be disinterested, no matter what the sacrifice. This led her to tell Reverend Hobart that if his friendship was the price for her fidelity to her beliefs, that was a price she would have to pay. She knew the pain that this separation would cause, yet in her honest search she was willing to live with that pain. In her journal she reflected:

[T]hey tell me I must worship him now in spirit and truth, but my poor spirit very often goes to sleep, or roves about like an idler for want of something to fix its attention, and for the truth...I feel more Union of heart and soul with him over a picture of the Crucifixion I found years ago in my Father's portfolio than in the—but what I was going to say would be folly, for truth *does not depend on the people around us or the place we are in, I can only say I do long and desire to worship our God in* Truth...[10]

With her vision so clouded, Elizabeth came to distrust her ability to articulate her experience. One who intimidated her was her brother-in-law, Wright Post. On one visit, when their conversation centered on her quandary about religious affiliation, she felt *"his cool and quiet Judgment, could not follow the flight of [her] Faith."*[11] And to his questioning she recalled her feeling of inadequacy: *"answered the poor, trembling Betsy Seton, dreading always to be pushed on the subject she could only feel, but never express to these coolest reasoners."*[12]

On the other side, she was torn by the prodding of Philip and Antonio Filicchi who questioned why she was equivocating now when earlier she seemed convinced. She found herself with no firm convictions and wondered when the storm would cease. The Scriptures, which were once her delight and comfort, were now sources of pain, every page "confounding" her poor soul.[13] She so wanted to follow God's will, if only she could see what it was for her, yet she felt there was *"a cloud before my way that keeps me from always* asking him *which is the right path."* [14] The images she uses express the extent of her frustration. She tells us, *"[M]y poor soul is...like a bird struggling in a net, it cannot escape its fear and trembling."* [15] *"[M]y Spirit lays in the Dust before God."* [16] *"[W]hen shall my darkness be made light...for indeed my spirit is sometimes so severely tried it is ready to sink."* [17]

Elizabeth's recourse in her inner turmoil was prayer and trust in God. She longed for light and knew it was only God's to give. A sampling of her reliance on God can instruct us on how we might traverse such a crisis in our own lives:

"I say to myself, be patient, God will bring you home at last." [18]

"At the foot of the cross I found consolation and kissing it over and over I repeated and repeat, There *only I am never disappointed...the poor Soul goes through nearly the same exercises day by day always drifting on the Ocean without any perceptible approach to its haven of rest but supported by its hope in God that he will never leave it to perish."* [19]

"...[M]y Soul cries out Jesus Jesus Jesus—there it finds rest, and heavenly Peace, and is hushed by that dear Sound as my little Babe is quieted by my cradle song." [20]

"[W]hen some hours of consolation come I think, hard as the trial is, yet it is sweet—I never knew what prayer is—never thought of fasting—though now it is more a habit than eating, never knew how to give up all, and send my spirit to mount [C]alvary nor how to console and delight it in the Society of Angels—Patience says my soul He will not let you and your little ones perish and, if yet your life is given in the conflict, at the last he will nail all to his cross and receive you to his mercy." [21]

Anyone who has ever been in the throes of a difficult decision can feel with Elizabeth how she returns to that same core: It is all in God's hands, there is no other recourse. After a seeming eternity of waiting, she reached a crisis. With an agonizing heart she read an Epiphany sermon about discerning the star of faith. In response she cried out, *"Alas, where is my star."*[22] In desperation she decided she must take action. She *looked straight up to God, and I told him since I cannot see the way to please you, whom alone I wish to please, every thing is indifferent to me, and until you do show me the way you mean for me to walk in I will trudge on in the path you suffered me to be born in,* taking herself to St. George Episcopal Church. As she participated in the services she was distressed at her lack of faith in them, *trembling to communion half dead...no words for her trial...but if I left the house a Protestant I returned to it a Catholick [sic] I think, since I determined to go no more to the Protestants.*[23]

By trying to force her decision, she confronted what was in the depths of her heart. A short time later she found herself peacefully and joyfully making her profession of faith in the Catholic Church. The turmoil of indecision was over. Relieved that her way was now clear, she wrote to Antonio Filicchi, *"I have been in a sea of troubles...but the guiding star was always bright and the master of the storm always in view."*[24]

Elizabeth is smiling as she recalls the joy she felt when the burden of indecision was lifted and she could *go peaceable and firmly to the Catholick [sic] church.* As she gazes at the rippling water, she tells us that the intensity of her desire to find God's will during her months of struggle left her with an unalterable commitment to an *entire abandonment to his will* for the rest of her life. And when those she loved faced important decisions she would offer them the benefit of her own experience by instructing them to *stay courageously in your station and wait until He makes [His will] clearly known to you.*[25]

With these final thoughts, she encourages us to spend

the rest of the day with our own experiences of searching for God's will. "Use your time today to reflect on how you are called to openness and patient waiting in such times," she suggests. "Rest peacefully in God's assurances of guidance and strength amid such struggles, when there seems to be a cloud before your path." As she finishes she moves off, walking thoughtfully along the creek.

For Reflection

- *Reflect on the images Elizabeth uses to describe her period of discernment. Write in a journal or draw images that describe times when you have endured a difficult decision-making experience.*

- *Spend time with Elizabeth's recounting of her frustration in trying to articulate her feelings to her brother-in-law whom she describes as a "cool reasoner." Recall how you have felt in similar circumstances and how, with prayer, you might respond differently.*

- *Reflect on Elizabeth's words: "Truth does not depend on the people around us or the place we are in." Does this prod you to any resolutions?*

- *How does Elizabeth's recounting of her struggle, "I never knew what prayer is—never thought of fasting," challenge you?*

Closing Prayer

Choose one or more of these paired passages from the word of God and the work of Elizabeth. Ask God to help you be aware of God's sustaining presence and support even in times of indecision.

From the word of God:

> Out of my distress I called on the LORD;
> the LORD answered me and set me in a broad place.
> With the LORD on my side, I do not fear.
> What can mortals do to me?
> The LORD is on my side to help me;
> I shall look in triumph on those who hate me
> (Psalm 118:5-7).

From the work of Elizabeth: *But oh my Father and my God.... Your word is truth, and without contradiction wherever it is, one Faith, one hope, one [B]aptism I look for, wherever it is...I will cling and hold to my God to the last gasp begging for that light and never change until I find it.*[26]

From the word of God:

> He...began to be grieved and agitated. Then he said to them, "I am deeply grieved, even to death...." And going a little farther, he threw himself on the ground and prayed, "My Father, if it is possible, let this cup pass from me; yet not what I want but what you want" (Matthew 26:37-39).

From the work of Elizabeth: *My heart feels so really bowed down that I cannot either fear or hope on the subject, but pray and fast, and try to keep both Eye and Soul fixed on God ready to meet his Will. Oh how eagerly they both stretch out to gain his blessed favor.*[27]

Notes

[1] Thomas Merton, *Thoughts in Solitude* (Garden City, N.Y.: Image Books, 1968), p. 81.

[2] Kelly and Melville, p. 150.

[3] Melville, p. 88.

[4] Kelly and Melville, p. 128.

[5] Kelly and Melville, p. 136.

[6] Melville, p. 117.

[7] Kelly and Melville, p. 349.

[8] Kelly and Melville, p. 144.

[9] Melville, p. 130.

[10] Kelly and Melville, p. 162.

[11] Kelly and Melville, p. 143.

[12] Dirvin, *Mrs. Seton*, p. 193.

[13] Kelly and Melville, p. 154.

[14] Kelly and Melville, p. 144.

[15] Kelly and Melville, p. 147.

[16] Kelly and Melville, p. 154.

[17] Kelly and Melville, p. 145.

[18] Madame De Barberey, *Elizabeth Seton* (New York: MacMillan Company, 1931), p. 122.

[19] Kelly and Melville, p. 150.

[20] Kelly and Melville, p. 148.

[21] Kelly and Melville, pp. 154-155.

[22] Kelly and Melville, p. 163.

[23] Kelly and Melville, p. 164.

[24] Kelly and Melville, p. 192.

[25] Kelly and Melville, p. 255.

[26] Kelly and Melville, p. 160.

[27] Kelly and Melville, p. 153.

Day Three
'My Soul's Sister'

Coming Together in the Spirit

A woman was making her way to a neighboring village, walking through a beautiful verdant valley. As she moved through the scene, she saw a farmer working his small plot. Periodically the farmer would stop, stand erect and whistle a little tune directed toward where the field sloped off over the hillside. The observer greeted him and remarked, "You seem to have a greater purpose in your whistling than simply enjoying the music."

"Ah, yes," the farmer smiled, "my home is just over the hill. My wife is there working at her chores of laundry and caring for our few animals. We have an agreement. Every time I think of her while I am in the field I whistle. She hears me and we know that our hearts are united. When she chimes the small bell hanging near our doorpost, I know she is signaling to me. Our tasks seem lighter as we recall that we are working, not alone, but in unison." This unison of hearts, even when apart from those we love, is a sure support as we go about our workaday world. When we find someone with whom we truly connect, with whom we are able to share our deepest selves, who we know really cares about us, we find ourselves feeling more alive.

Defining Our Thematic Context

On Day Two Elizabeth accompanied us in an exploration of the struggle we sometimes encounter when faced with a difficult decision. By her example she showed us the costs involved in choices we might need to make in integrity to our inner spirit. In the final analysis, trust and abandonment to God's will are our only recourse, as much as we might wish to bring our state of uncertainty to a hasty conclusion. Only in God's good time will peace and light become ours again.

Today our mentor will help us explore the riches of spiritual relationships. For Elizabeth, all relationships were spiritual, and she experienced great joy and interior growth by giving deeply of herself. Cultivating trust and finding ways of affirming and continually deepening a union of hearts are challenges for each of us. The rewards are great, however, especially when they draw us into deeper communion with God.

Opening Prayer

Jesus, in your life you developed deep and enriching
   friendships. You knew the joys of sharing and
   mutual support that were present in your
   relationships with Lazarus, with Mary Magdalen
   and with your Beloved Disciple. I thank you for the
   special relationships in my life:
for the joy of deep exchanges,
   for the mutuality of caring,
   for the blessing of common experiences and shared
      interests,
   for the opportunities for growth,
   for the risks I find myself willing to take for another,

for the pain which can be shared,
for the support which buoys me in low times,
for the face of you I see in the other.
I ask you for the patience and generosity necessary to
foster and sustain such relationships. May they
always be freely given and freely received, and may
they always lead me to a deeper friendship with
you. Amen.

Retreat Session Three

"Recollections of sunrises and sunsets—that's what
we're going to pray with today," says our mentor.
"Because friends are like sunsets and sunrises. They are
experiences of transcendence that come to us as gifts,
sometimes most unexpectantly. They lift our spirits
beyond ourselves, often to God, and become part of the
core of who we are. They carry us forward into greater
potential for awareness of all of life, and give us
endearing memories." It is fitting that Elizabeth has
gathered us in a beautiful grove of mature trees diffusing
the sunlight, a serene setting which induces us to reach
into our memories of times shared.

"I pray that each of you receives the treasure of an
intimate friendship, especially one that is built on and
nourishes your passion for God," she comments. "So
often I am reminded of special moments shared with
another when I am engrossed in nature. And my heart is
encouraged by those recollections. Nature is a setting
conducive to drawing out what is deepest within us."

"Let's start our time together today with a little quiz,"
she teasingly challenges. "Call to mind a friend who is

close at hand. When was the last time you had a 'soul sharing'?"

After a pause, as if offering encouragement for our reflection, she whispers, "*My heart melts at the thought of how dear we are to each other and the tie which binds us.*"[1]

"Think about a friend who is at a distance. What have you done to nurture that relationship, to keep it alive?"

And then she comments, "*There is no distance for souls and mine has surely been with yours most faithfully.*"[2]

"Recall a friend from bygone times. What have you learned that might have made your friendship richer?"

After a period of quiet she proposes: "*My darling soul, think of him, love him and look to him and never mind the rest—all will be well.*"[3]

Elizabeth was blessed with intimate friendships all of her adult life. Her outgoing nature created an openness around her which welcomed others and encouraged them to blossom in her presence. She exuded a sincere reverence which assured others they were accepted and appreciated for who they were. And, she was unwilling to allow past differences to create lasting barriers. For instance, despite a family rift with her stepmother and a coolness from family members after her conversion to Catholicism, Elizabeth *had the indescribable satisfaction*[4] of being called to nurse her half-sister Emma, as well as her stepmother in their last illnesses.

She sustained a self-revealing and voluminous correspondence at great personal price: The usual time she squeezed this practice into her busy life was after the rest of the house had retired. In addition, she kept journals recording some of the most memorable periods in her life for the benefit of her closest friends. In these she shared the joys and sorrows of the everyday as well as her most intimate prayer experiences. She delighted in the company of others. Imagine her friends' response when encouraged to visit by such invitations as:

"The front door, the back door, the side door which will lead her to the chapel, and all the windows up and down will open at your approach."[5]

"The rays of the sun, which I welcome in such a pleasant manner when they flit across my windows are no more welcome than your well-known steps at my door."[6]

As Elizabeth yearned to know and love others, she sought these same things for herself. Her ability to bring a focused attentiveness to others assured them of their value and of her love for them. She identified with the pain of others and was vulnerable in allowing others to share hers. And she clearly saw the mutual nurturing which friendship brought about as strongly connected with knowing and being known by God in an ever-deepening way. She once commented to a friend:

"Religion does not limit the powers of the affections, for our Blessed Saviour sanctifies and approves in us all the endearing ties and connections of our existence. But religion alone can bind that cord over which neither circumstances, time, nor death, can have power."[7]

One of the most intimate of Elizabeth's relationships was that which she shared with her sister-in-law, Rebecca Seton. Like the growth cycle of a young tree, their friendship developed from bud, to delicate lacy sprout, to mature green fullness. Elizabeth first came to know "Bec" when she was but a teenager, and Elizabeth a young bride. At first Elizabeth regarded her as a person with good, but neglected qualities. Later, the two became members of a society to aid destitute widows with children and spent many hours sharing this work. With the death of the elder Mr. Seton, they were thrown together in the same household, sharing responsibility for Bec's younger siblings. It was through these seasons of life that they grew in their love and appreciation of each

other's qualities. They began to share the substance of
their lives with each other. As Anne Morrow Lindbergh
reminded us:

> [The web of love] is made of loyalties, and
> interdependencies, and shared experiences. It is
> woven of memories of meetings and conflicts; of
> triumphs and disappointments. It is a web of
> communication, a common language, and the
> acceptance of lack of language too; a knowledge of
> likes and dislikes, of habits and reactions, both
> physical and mental. It is a web of instincts and
> intuitions, and known and unknown exchanges.[8]

During a winter when Bec was away for reasons of
health, Elizabeth wistfully described the depth of her
loneliness:

*"I never sweep the hall, or dress the flower pots, or walk
around the pear-tree walk, but you are as much my companion
as if you were actually near me, and last evening finding myself
accidentally by the garden fence at the head of the lane where
we once stood at sunset last Fall...I was so struck with the
recollection and the uncertainty of when I should see you again,
that I had a hearty crying spell, which is not a very common
thing for me."*[9]

Bec, in turn, wrote to her, "The idea of my spending
the winter away from you makes me miserable."[10]

As their love deepened, these "soul sisters" grew in
their own self-discovery. They found safe haven in a
climate of trust and of mutual self-revelation. They shared
their weaknesses, fears and deep inner longings, and
came to accept each other in their faults and limitations. It
was during these years that Bec was suffering serious
bouts with tuberculosis. At the same time the Seton family
business was floundering and William Seton's health was
worsening as well. When circumstances forced her to be
separated from Bec, Elizabeth grieved at the loss of this

precious support and felt that her *"circle has lost its key."* [11]

The two developed such a strong support system that being apart left a deep void. Elizabeth confided to Bec, *"You cannot know my sister the melancholy thoughts that press on [me] whenever I consider myself without you in Stone Street, it seems to me as if I could as soon enjoy Home without limb or a part of myself. This no one else can understand, but I am sure you do."* [12]

And during the summer when Elizabeth spent her time away from the city, she sent endearing notes telling of each day's events, the activities of the children and spiritual insights to *my darling Soul's Sister.* [13]

How are you employed my own Rebecca, and how have I been employed?...but there is no distance for Souls and mine has surely been with yours most faithfully—St. Paul's Steeple, Rebecca and [Henry Hobart] were thought of...dear, dear Rebecca how I long to see you.

My own Rebecca how much I wish you were here to enjoy this beautiful sunset at the corner of the Piazza.... My Father...calls Cate Aunt Rebecca and all the family have found out that she is your image—I pray that she may be both in the interior as well as the exterior.

A bright sun and every blessing surrounding me...this day [my soul] flys to Him the merciful giver of this unspeakable blessing.

Sweet Peace is strongest this day, the sun set last Evening without a cloud...did you ever experience the awe (tho I know you have) Solemn though greatly heightened by viewing the Heavens in open space without an intervening object.

I am in truth your own Sister. E.A.S. [14]

As prayerful women, Elizabeth and Bec thrived on and shared their enthusiasm for religious practices despite snickering from less ardent friends and relatives. Attending Sunday services together, they would press each other's arms and sigh when they turned from the church door, knowing they would not come again until the following week. And on Sacrament Sundays they were laughed at for running from one church to another in order to receive Communion as often as they could.[15]

During her ill-fated trip to Italy in 1803, Elizabeth kept a journal for Rebecca in which she poured out her soul, sharing the turmoil, fear and divine strength the traveler experienced during her months abroad. Amidst her difficult sojourn, Elizabeth's "soul cried out for those she loved," as she reminisced about "all the things they used to do together": their many "looks exchanged" and "sunsets shared." And she "longed for the day when they would be together again." This spiritual journal opens Elizabeth's soul as she shares her intimate moments with her dying husband as well as her most profound prayers with *the dear Companion of all the pains—and all the comforts—of Songs of Praise and notes of sorrow, the dear, faithful, tender friend of my Soul through every varied scene.*[16]

Always ardently devoted to belief in Christ's presence in the Eucharist, during her month-long confinement with her sick husband in Italy, Elizabeth longed for union with God and her friend. She calculated the time those at home would be receiving the Sacrament and resolved to enter into spiritual communion in order to meet them in spirit.[17] It is no wonder then that Elizabeth longed to share her new-found awareness of Catholic belief in the Real Presence with Rebecca. She was the only one Elizabeth implicitly trusted to listen profoundly, understand and share her awe, her questions and her search for *truth*. Now she exclaims to Rebecca in her journal:

"My Rebecca My Soul's Sister—how many thoughts and affections pass my mind in a day, and you so far away to whom I would wish to tell all—

"I don't know how to say the awful effect at being where

they told me God was present in the blessed sacrament.

"My sister dear how happy would we be if we believed what these dear souls believe, that they possess God *in the Sacrament and that he remains in their churches and is carried to them when they are sick...."*[18]

Elizabeth was sorely disappointed, upon her return from Italy, to find Bec too ill to meet her at the dock. The dying woman's weakness and constant pain prevented the happy reunion which Elizabeth had anticipated. Even so, in their final few weeks, they reached a dimension of sharing unimaginable to less generous souls. Elizabeth revealed her new-found faith and Bec, in her weakness, could only repeat, "Your people are my people, Your God My God."[19] On the day of Rebecca's death, only a few weeks later, Elizabeth addressed her dearest friend,

"[D]ear dear Soul we shall no more watch the setting sun on our knees and sigh our soul to the Sun of Righteousness, for he has received you to his everlasting light—no more singing praises gazing on the moon—for you have awakened to eternal day—that dear voice that soothed the widow's heart, admonished the forgetful Soul, inspired the love of God, and only uttered sounds of love and peace to all shall now be heard no more among us.... He who searches the heart and knows the spring of each secret affection—He only knows what I lost at that moment."[20]

As she finishes, Elizabeth's eyes are reflecting the joy of recalling such a deep love shared. She quietly leaves us with the challenge of examining the quality of our own relationships. "Be assured," she asserts, "if God blesses you with an opportunity for such friendship, you must embrace it, for it is a sure path to deeper union with God."

For Reflection

- *In a society which values individualism and personal space, what do you communicate to others by the way you receive them into your presence? What do you communicate to others by the efforts you place on staying in touch?*

- *Keeping a journal for a friend was a favorite way of Elizabeth's to share the depths of her experiences. Have you ever kept a journal for a friend? Consider this as a way of enriching a friendship.*

- *Reflect on a time when "your circle had lost its key." Journal about how you felt or responded.*

- *List qualities you feel most comfortable with in others. Are these models for incorporation into your own dealings with others?*

Closing Prayer

Choose one or more of these paired passages from the word of God and the work of Elizabeth Seton. Ask God for the special grace of friendships that both enrich and challenge you.

From the word of God:

But Mary stood weeping outside the tomb. As she wept, she bent over to look into the tomb; ...she turned around and saw Jesus standing there, but she did not know that it was Jesus. Jesus said to her, "Woman, why are you weeping? Whom are you looking for?" Supposing him to be the gardener, she said to him, "Sir, if you have carried him away, tell me where you have laid him, and I will take him away." Jesus said to her, "Mary!" She turned and said to him in Hebrew, "Rabbouni!" (which means Teacher). Jesus said to her, "Do not hold on to me...." (John 20:11, 14-17).

From the work of Elizabeth: *My heart melts at the thought of how dear we are to each other and the tie which binds us.*[21]

From the word of God:

In those days Mary set out and went with haste to a Judean town in the hill country, where she entered the house of Zechariah and greeted Elizabeth. When Elizabeth heard Mary's greeting, the child leaped in her womb. And Elizabeth was filled with the Holy Spirit... (Luke 1:39-41).

From the work of Elizabeth: *I carry you constantly in my heart before him who loves us, and so much more than any friend can love a friend.*[22]

Notes

[1] Elizabeth Seton to Cecilia Seton, undated note, Archives St. Joseph Provincial House, ASJPH 1-3-3-8:143.

[2] Kelly and Melville, p. 75.

[3] Elizabeth Seton to Cecilia Seton, 1 July 1807, Archives St. Joseph Provincial House, ASJPH 1-3-3-8:138.

[4] Code, p. 132.

[5] Melville, p. 258.

[6] De Barbery, p. 444.

[7] Code, p. 104.

[8] Anne Morrow Lindbergh, *Gift From the Sea* (New York: Vintage Books, 1978), p. 82.

[9] Melville, p. 60.

[10] Melville, p. 60.

[11] Melville, p. 81.

[12] Elizabeth Seton to Rebecca Seton, 10 July 1799, Archives of the Sisters of Charity of Seton Hill #7-10.

[13] Kelly and Melville, p. 78.

[14] Kelly and Melville, pp. 75-78.

[15] Kelly and Melville, pp. 134-135.

[16] Kelly and Melville, p. 136.

[17] Kelly and Melville, pp. 116-117.

[18] Kelly and Melville, pp. 130-133.

[19] Kelly and Melville, p. 349.

[20] Kelly and Melville, pp. 137, 138.

[21] Elizabeth Seton to Cecilia Seton, undated note, Archives St. Joseph Provincial House ASJPH 1-3-3-8:143.

[22] Code, p. 163.

DAY FOUR
A Parent's Unconditional Love

Coming Together in the Spirit

The excitement that it was a beautiful, blond baby boy was soon overshadowed by concerned inquiries: "Is something wrong with Jeff?" Numerous trips to doctors confirmed that, indeed, Jeff was one of God's "special children."

Amidst the heartache and struggles, however, this charming little boy wound himself around everyone's heart. Cathy and Jim, his parents, spent endless hours and resources seeking any way to improve his chances for development. Priorities were changed, life-styles and schedules were juggled. Relatives and friends were enlisted to work with Jeff on physical patterning and intellectual stimulation. Moments of hope were mixed with tears of disappointment. But the love poured out by Jeff's family was never a question. He became "wrapped in the very nerves of our souls."[1]

Defining Our Thematic Context

On Day Three Elizabeth shared the wealth of her own intimate relationships with us. As in the case of Rebecca, the soul-sharing in which the two engaged was a priceless pearl for each of them. In her connections, one of our director's deepest longings was to see her friend drawn into closer intimacy with God, and in this way to deepen their own relationship. Reflecting on Elizabeth's experiences, she challenged us to examine the quality of our own relationships.

Today we are invited to consider the topic of parenting. From her earliest years Elizabeth was attracted to the image of God as her Father. Later she grew to recognize and love Mary as her heavenly mother. These spiritual relationships proved to be models for her own parenting. Motherhood is a place where she met her grace in a most fulfilling way. She thrived on walking with her children through each step of their lives yet was able to release them to their own destinies blessed with her unconditional love.

Opening Prayer

Remember, O most gracious virgin Mary, that never was it known that anyone who fled to your protection, implored your help or sought your intercession was left unaided. Inspired by this confidence I fly unto you O virgin of virgins, my mother. To you I come, before you I stand sinful and sorrowful. O mother of the Word Incarnate, despise not my petitions but in your mercy hear and answer me. Amen.

—*Memorare of Saint Bernard*

RETREAT SESSION FOUR

We were surprised not to find our enthusiastic mentor waiting at our appointed place. Then we glimpsed her strolling toward us arm-in-arm with a younger woman. As they drew near, their unmistakable resemblance was evident. Beaming, our director says, "I am delighted to introduce you to my daughter, Kit. She's going to join us today. I think she may have something to add to our gathering."

Kit smiles brightly as the sweep of her gaze greets each of us in turn. Her mannerisms and gestures are reminiscent of her mother. With a sideways glance at Elizabeth she declares, "When my mother told me the topic today was parenting, I volunteered to appear as an 'expert witness!' Our home was a wonderful, nurturing place for my sisters and brothers and me." She rushes on, "Even in stressful times when things were going badly we knew we were loved beyond measure. I remember as a small child singing and dancing around the piano, reading by the fire and welcoming friends and relatives to our circle. There was always room for one more, and...."

"Wait, wait!" Elizabeth laughingly interrupts. "Let me get us started in a little different direction." She smiles knowingly to herself and then says: "You often hear me referred to as 'Mother Seton,' which is usually by way of a religious title. But to me, being a 'mother'—either physically *or* spiritually—is my calling from God. It is in this role that I flourished and grew as a person and in my relationship with God."

Elizabeth had little early modeling for a role that was to become so central to her life. Saddened at the early loss of her mother and deprived by her father's frequent absences, the young girl developed a deep sense of God's

protective presence. In later life she recalled such a time
when she was enjoying a spring day in the woods at the
age of fourteen:

*...the sweet clovers and wild flowers I had got by the way,
and a heart as innocent as a human heart could be, filled with
even enthusiastic love to God and admiration of his works—
still I can feel every sensation that passed thro' my Soul—I
thought at the time my Father did not care for me—well God
was my Father—my All. I prayed—sung hymns—cryed—
laughed in talking to myself of how far He could place me
above all Sorrow.*[2]

Despite his absences, Elizabeth loved and idolized her
father. He responded in turn with a deep affection. He
saw to her education and provided his daughter with
opportunities to develop her many talents. After her
marriage he became a frequent visitor to her home and
delighted in his grandchildren. Summers shared at his
Staten Island cottage were precious times for the devoted
daughter. They remained treasured memories throughout
her life. On her watch chain she wore a gold cross which
her father had given her. It served as a reminder to her of
both him and what it symbolized. And, as she matured,
she emulated many of his values, notably his concern for
and dedication to those most in need.

Elizabeth's joy in married life was only magnified
with the arrival of her children, who came in quick
succession. She was the mother of five within seven and a
half years of marriage, and in her way of reckoning, each
child was born to be treasured. Her first, Anna Maria
(Annina), was from the beginning her companion and
comfort. Two sons, William and Richard, followed. Both
were sources of delight as well as concern to their mother
as they sought to find their ways in the world. Catherine
(Kit) and Rebecca were the youngest, and to their doting
mother, the brightest of the lot. From the start Elizabeth's

children "wound themselves around her heart."

The very qualities of Elizabeth's personality made her enjoy every aspect of motherhood. Her warmth, effusiveness and ease with physical and psychological intimacy found perfect outlets in her bonding with her children. The close family circle that she yearned for as a child became a reality. For the joy-filled young mother, happiness centered in her home. She relished the cheerful fire and the camaraderie; the peacefulness and the security. Music, storytelling, walks and other simple pleasures were all she yearned for. She exulted in time spent with her children and enjoyed seeing them romping knee-deep in clover or playing "tea" with little shells gathered along the shore. In one note to her sister-in-law, Rebecca, she recounted:

"I have cut out my two suits today and partly made one— Heard all the lessons too...And should I complain with a bright moon over my shoulder and the darlings all well, hallooing and dancing?—I have played for them this half hour."[3]

And in a letter to her friend, Julia Scott, she commented:

"For myself, I think the greatest happiness of this life is to be released from the cares and formalities of what is called the world. My world is my family and all the change to me will be that I can devote myself unmolested to my treasure."[4]

Her enthusiasm for her children can be seen in her anxiousness to share them with friends and relatives by providing every detail of their childhood antics or inviting as many as five people to stand as godparents at a christening.

Content as she was on one level with her precious gifts from God, on another she harbored a lingering concern. Again and again she expressed her desire that they would always be pleasing to their heavenly Father:

"Anina a thousand times offered and given up while in her

innocence fearing so much she would live and be lost—daily entreaties to God to take whom he pleased, or all *if he pleased, only not to lose him....*

"*Continual offering up my sweet Anna and William and Richard and Catherine and little Bec from their first entrance into the world—fear of their* Eternal loss *the prevailing care through all the pains or pleasures of a Mother.*"[5]

And at a later time after receiving Communion, she articulated her deep sense of connection with both her daughter and her God:

Received the longing Desire of my soul, and my dearest Anna too. The bonds of nature and grace all twined together. The parent offers the child, the child the parent, and both are united in the source of their being, and rest together on redeeming love.[6]

Elizabeth had always looked to God as her loving parent, but as turmoil and crisis invaded her life, this relationship became even more important. Again and again during her husband's last agony and during her conversion struggle she cried out to God as her Father, exclaiming, "*If I could forget my God one moment at these times I should go mad—but He hushes all—Be still and know that I am God your Father.*"[7] And after her husband's death repeating the prayer, "*...my God you are my God, and so I am now alone in the world with you and my little ones but you are my father and doubly theirs.*"[8]

On her return to New York after a nine-month absence from her four youngest children, she recounted the bittersweet moment:

"*Do I hold my dear ones again in my bosom—has God restored* all *my Treasure.... Nature crys out they are Fatherless—while God himself replies I am the Father of the Fatherless and the helper of the helpless—My God well may I cling to thee for "whom have I in Heaven but thee and who upon Earth beside thee, My heart and my flesh fail but thou art the Strength of my heart and my portion forever.*"[9]

While circumstances reinforced her fidelity to God as her father, Elizabeth was, at the same time, gifted with a whole new relationship in the midst of her sorrow. While in Italy, *[a] little prayer-book of Mrs. F[ilicchi]'s was on the table, and I opened [to] a little prayer of St. Bernard to the Blessed Virgin, begging her to be* our Mother; *and I said to her, with such a certainty that God would surely refuse nothing to His Mother, and that she could not help loving and pitying the poor souls he died for, that I felt really I had a Mother— which you know my foolish heart so often lamented to have lost in early days. From the first remembrance of infancy I have looked, in all the plays of childhood and wildness of youth, to the clouds for my mother; and at that moment it seemed as if I had found more than her, even in tenderness and pity of a mother. So I cried myself to sleep on her heart.*[10]

From that time Elizabeth established lasting rapport with the mother of Jesus. She sensed that Mary would respond with solicitude to her bereavement and identify with the joys and sorrows Elizabeth experienced in raising her children. During her adjustment to life as a single parent struggling to make ends meet, her newfound mother came to occupy a central role both for her and for her children. She recalled:

"Our first hail Mary in our little closet at night prayers when Nina said oh Ma let us say hail Mary, do ma said Willy, and hail Mary we all said, little Bec looking in my face to catch the words she could not pronounce but in a manner which would have made all laugh if Mother's tears had not fixed their attention."[11]

Elizabeth used the models of God as Father and Mary as mother to deepen her own prayer life as well. In one meditation she reflected on the example of her own daughter's devotion to her as a spur to her relationship with God:

*"Beloved Kate, I will take you then, for my pattern and try
to please Him as you to please me. To grieve with a like
tenderness when I displease* Him, *to obey and mind His voice
as you do mine. To do my work as neatly and exactly as you do
yours, grieve to lose sight of Him for a moment, fly with joy to
meet Him, fear He should go and leave me even when I sleep—
this is the lesson of love you set me. And when I have seemed to
be angry, without petulance or obstinacy you silently and
steadily try to accomplish my wish, I will say: "Dearest Lord,
give me grace to copy well this lovely image of my duty to
Thee."*[12]

In another she entered into Mary's experience as
mother, in order to appreciate more deeply the mysteries
of the Incarnation. On the feast of the Assumption 1813,
she meditated on the wonders of this mother/son
relationship in light of her own mothering experiences:

*Jesus nine months in Mary, feeding on her blood—Oh,
Mary! These nine months. Jesus on the breast of Mary, feeding
on her milk! How she must have delayed the weaning of such a
child!!!! The infancy of Jesus—in her lap—on her knees as on
His throne.... The youth, the obscure life, the public life of Jesus.
Mary always, everywhere, in every moment, day and night,
conscious she was His Mother! Oh, glorious, happy Mother,
even through the sufferings and ignominies of her Son. Her full
conformity to Him—O virtues of Mary—the constant delight
of the Blessed Trinity—she alone giving Them more glory than
all heaven together. Mother of God! Mary! Oh, the purity of
Mary! The humility, patience, love, of Mary!—to imitate at
humblest distance.*[13]

Using these two strong models Elizabeth built her
patterns of relating to her own children. To them she
communicated her most deeply held values, teaching
more by her presence and her example than by any
instruction.

Kit is radiant as she recalls the loving climate that

prevailed within her family. "Like Mary to Jesus, we were all so devoted to each other," she recalls. "Of course, that's what we learned at my mother's knee. None of us ever doubted her uncompromising love. Every decision she made placed our needs first."

"One thing that I found hard," interjects the mother, "was balancing my tendency to be protective with the letting go needed as each of you grew older. And, of course, the separations, which were part of the letting go."

"Yes," Kit responds, "the separations were hard. With the boys leaving for school and careers. We missed them so. And life itself so tenuous, especially with my sisters becoming victims of tuberculosis."

"But through it all I know how blessed I was," comments Elizabeth feelingly. "I love my special God-given charges more than I can describe. Even amidst the pain they are my greatest joy. Experiencing God's unconditional love for me and using Mary as a model of parenthood, I am able to place all events within the eternal plan. And now I invite all of you to quietly consider your own experience of God's parenting. I pray the prayer I said at my youngest daughter's Baptism— this time for all of you.

May you receive the fullness of His grace and remain in the number of His faithful children—that being steadfast in the faith, joyful through hope and rooted in charity, you may so pass the waves of this troublesome world that finally you may enter the land of everlasting life.[14]

For Reflection

- *Elizabeth developed a practice of taking short reflection periods even in the midst of a busy day surrounded by her children. She found these "tiny islands of solitude and grace" helped her to place all events in the context of the eternal plan. What steps might you take to cultivate this pattern?*

- *When referring to her children Elizabeth noted, "Nature's plants are indeed various." She loved and valued each of them in her/his uniqueness, appreciating God's gifts as manifested in each one. In what circumstances in your life are you challenged to love and value another's uniqueness? Name someone who presents this challenge for you. How might you become more open?*

- *Considering Elizabeth's discovery of Mary as a true mother to her, reflect on your own relationship with Mary. How might you develop this more fully in order to move more deeply into the mystery of the Incarnation?*

- *Choose a tape of a song reflecting God's love as a parent (i.e., "Isaiah 49" or "On Eagle's Wings"). Spend a prayer period in quiet contemplation of the music and the message.*

Closing Prayer

Choose one or more of these paired passages from the word of God and from the work of Elizabeth Seton. Ask God, as a loving parent, to increase your sense of trust.

From the word of God:

You have seen what I did...how I bore you on eagles' wings and brought you to myself (Exodus 19:4).

From the work of Elizabeth: *Is it nothing to sleep secure under His guardian wing—to awake to the brightness of the* *glorious sun with renewed strength and renewed blessing—to be blessed with the power of instant communion with the Father of our spirits, the sense of His presence—the influences of His love?*[15]

Mary Queen and Virgin pure!—as poor unfledged Birds uncovered in our cold and hard nests on this earth we cry to her for her sheltering outspread wings—little hearts not yet knowing sorrow—but poor tired and older ones pressed with pains and cares seek peace and rest—O our Mother! And find it in thee.[16]

From the word of God:

> ...I tell you, do not worry about your life, what you will eat or what you will drink, or about your body, what you will wear.... Look at the birds of the air; they neither sow nor reap nor gather into barns, and yet your heavenly Father feeds them. Are you not of more value than they? (Matthew 6:25-26).

From the work of Elizabeth: *All my little flock were resting peaceably within the fold. Well might their mother arise to acknowledge, to praise, and to bless the gracious Shepherd who preserves them safely in His refuge, feeds them with His hand, and leads them to the refreshing stream. Well may she follow on, confiding them to His care, rejoicing in His presence, triumphing in His protection and seeking only to express her grateful joy and love, but seeking His favor by submission to His will.*[17]

Notes

[1] Jack Canfield and Mark Victor Hansen, *Chicken Soup for the Soul* (Deerfield Beach, Fla.: Health Communications Inc., 1993), p. 8.

[2] Kelly and Melville, p. 115.

[3] Joseph I. Dirvin, *The Soul of Elizabeth Seton* (San Francisco: Ignatius Press, 1990), p. 91.

[4] Melville, p. 75.

[5] Kelly and Melville, pp. 346-347.

[6] Dirvin, *Soul*, p. 75.

[7] Kelly and Melville, p. 109.

[8] Kelly and Melville, p. 130.

[9] Kelly and Melville, p. 136.

[10] Dirvin, *Soul*, p. 79.

[11] Kelly and Melville, p. 350.

[12] Dirvin, *Soul*, p. 75.

[13] Dirvin, *Soul*, p. 83.

[14] Sister Marie Celeste, S.C., *Elizabeth Ann Seton: A Woman of Prayer* (New York: Alba House, 1993), p. 13.

[15] Celeste, p. 9.

[16] Kelly and Melville, p. 331.

[17] Celeste, p. 18.

DAY FIVE
'Mother of Many Daughters'

Coming Together in the Spirit

It happened when Elaine Prevallet was a nineteen-year-old college junior. She was in her dorm room one night trying to read an assignment. But her mind kept wandering off, refusing to heed the book. So Prevallet put the book down and listened. The message came through "large as a neon sign, loud as a boombox in full volume" right in her ear.

"You have to be a nun."

The young student was startled. Not given to voices or visions, she was caught totally off guard. Yet she could not ignore it—two years later she entered the convent. She could empathize with Saint Augustine who, in his *Confessions*, had admitted: "My inner self was a house divided against itself.... There are two wills in us, because neither by itself is the whole will, and each possesses what the other lacks."[1]

Despite her doubts and natural aversion to convent life in the beginning, Elaine Prevallet remained faithful to the message. She kept moving further into God's will. Forty years later, looking back at her early resistance to the life she came to love, she observed, "God only calls us to be who we are."[2]

Defining Our Thematic Context

Yesterday Elizabeth disclosed to us her own reliance on God as divine parent and Mary as her heavenly mother. These relationships nourished her prayer and inspired her own parenting. They enabled her to bestow uncompromising, self-forgetful love on her children. Our mentor encouraged us to learn from God and from our own children how to love faithfully and well.

Today we will explore how Elizabeth's role in the founding of the Sisters of Charity in the United States reflects one of the great themes of her spirituality: finding the will of God in the unfolding events of her life. In the process of giving herself over to listening and waiting for God, the recent convert found herself in the unlikely role of religious superior and spiritual mentor to aspiring women religious. God was full of surprises!

Opening Prayer

Time has one song alone. If you are heedful
and concentrate on sound with all your soul,
you may hear the song of the beautiful will of God,
soft notes or deep sonorous tones that roll
like thunder over time.
Not many have the hearing for this music,
and fewer still have sought it as sublime.
Listen, and tell your grief: But God is singing!
God sings through all creation with His will.
Save the negation of sin, all is His music,
even the notes that set their roots in ill
to flower in pity, pardon or sweet humbling.
Evil finds harshness of the rack and rod
in tunes where good finds tenderness and glory.
The saints who loved have died of this pure music,

and no one enters heaven till he learns,
deep in his soul at least, to sing with God.[3]

RETREAT SESSION FIVE

Today we gather on the shady lawn outside the old
"Stone House." From this vantage we can see the expanse
of St. Joseph's Valley and beyond to the tree-covered
mountains which rise from the valley floor. Elizabeth is
there to meet us and the glow on her face indicates that
this setting holds a special significance for her.

"This very building," she announces, "is the cradle
where the Sisters of Charity were nourished." By this
point in our time together her gentle enthusiasm has
become both familiar and contagious among the
retreatants. Each day we anticipate our appointed time to
come under the tutelage of this warm and embracing
woman, anxious to enjoy her presence as well as to share
more of her story and nourish our own prayer life.

"Can you imagine a more beautiful and peaceful
setting?" she continues. "But arriving at this place was
not by any means a clear and straight path. As you can
imagine, my journey from New York to Emmitsburg was
far more than a physical relocation. As I told a friend
during this time, *they do not know what to do with me*, but
God does—*and when His blessed time is come we shall know.*[4]

"Searching for the will of God or waiting for it to
become manifest is often difficult," our mentor reminds
us. "We want to take things into our own hands and
make them happen. Instead we must learn to be open,
wait, and be ready for surprises. Often these times are
turning points in our lives. I urge you to reflect on pivotal

times in your own life."

After Elizabeth's conversion to Catholicism she was faced with opposition from relatives and friends as well as the practical necessity of caring for herself and her five young children. Her life was in turmoil and of necessity would take a whole new direction. What that was to be, remained unclear. Those who were trying to assist her had many suggestions ranging from becoming the proprietor of a tea store or a china shop, to opening a school for small children, to taking in students as boarders. The projects in which she did become involved came to naught. In the midst of this stress, though, she held to a firm trust that God was close by leading and guiding her. Step by step she explored various possibilities and ultimately found herself in a quite unanticipated place.

One proposal Elizabeth initially found attractive was to send her boys to school in the Catholic atmosphere of Montreal. She even entertained the distant hope that she and her girls might be received in a convent there where she could find peace while making herself useful as an assistant teacher. But, she reflected, *[f]or myself—certainly the only fear I can have is that there is too much of self seeking in pleading for accomplishment of this object which however I joyfully yield to the Will of the Almighty, confident that as he has disposed my Heart to wish above all things to please Him, it will not be disappointed in the desire whatever may be his appointed means.*[5]

And one of her advisers counseled: "God has His moments which we need not anticipate, and prudent slowness only ripens and brings to fruition the good desires which Grace inspires within us."[6]

Elizabeth herself saw little hope of the Canadian plan coming to fruition when she wrote, "*God will direct it—and that is enough...according to the old rule I look neither behind nor before but straight upwards, without thinking of human calculations... it* all *belongs to God."*[7]

And in a later letter, when reflecting on the contradictions in which she was living, she commented, *"these are my happiest days...[I am] convinced this is the day of salvation for me and if like a coward I should run away from the field of battle I am sure the very Peace I seek would fly from me, and the state of Penance sanctified by the will of God would be again wished for as the safest and surest road."*[8]

After three long years of frustrating uncertainty Elizabeth received an invitation to open a school in Baltimore. Suddenly things fell together and within a matter of months she found herself embraced by the Catholic community of that city. She enthusiastically commented about her new circumstances: *"Doubt and fear fly from the breast inhabited by him—there can be no disappointment where the Souls only desire and expectation is to meet his Adored Will and fulfill it."*[9]

Events unfolded quickly for Elizabeth after her arrival in Baltimore. She soon found herself not only the director of a school but the head of a nascent religious community when young women from around the country were directed to join her. The evolution of the group was a gradual process unfolding with the passing months. Of course these new circumstances brought concerns and decisions of their own: how to establish a financial base, where to locate the foundation, what rule of life to adopt. All were difficult to make, but the new foundress plunged forward with her characteristic approach, writing to Bishop John Carroll, *"now I am going straight on by Faith...I abandon myself to God continually and invite all my dear companions to do the same."*[10]

And to her sister-in-law, Cecilia, *"There can be no disappointment where the soul's only desire and expectation is to meet His adored Will and fulfill it."*[11]

Of all the new challenges her new way of life presented, perhaps the most humbling for Elizabeth was assuming the role of superior of the new community. She felt a sense of unworthiness for such an awesome task and doubted her own ability to do the job. Her first companion in the community expressed surprise at the "alarm" Elizabeth felt at taking on these duties and assured her that "Jesus can never give you a task above your courage, strength or ability."[12]

Yet for a time the task did seem overwhelming to the foundress. She chafed under decisions and modes of governing imposed upon her by superiors and confessed to Bishop Carroll that she had "been made a Mother before being initiated."[13] She told him that "circumstances have all so combined as to create in my mind a confusion and want of confidence in my Superiors which is indescribable."[14] She struggled to bend to their will but found it impossible admitting that she did not possess the "pliancy of character" required. [T]he fire of tribulation...has at times burnt so deep that the anguish could not be concealed; but by degrees custom reconciles pain itself, and I determine, dry and hard as my daily bread is, to take it with as good grace as possible.[15]

Bishop Carroll stood by her during this difficult period and over time circumstances took care of themselves.

Even in the midst of turbulent beginnings, Elizabeth's companions took to her charismatic leadership and she to her role as religious mentor. The ties established within the group were described by the sisters as those of a "blessed family" who were "but one heart and one soul." Her letters to them are filled with exclamations of her heartfelt regard for them. To a friend in New York she wrote, "you may suppose what...[they] are to my heart after so many years of care and pains and comfort together."[16] And when several returned from mission she effused, "Such a pleasure to have Cis and Fan home again, it is new life to me."[17]

Elizabeth was regarded as both mother and sister by her companions. With some she exchanged intimate and challenging letters containing mutual encouragement and urges to greater perfection. To one she wrote, *"how often did we not agree that...it was better to go on, and take the abundant sweet heavenly grace from day to day, only seeking and seeing him in all our little duties (so small an offering)— and taking from the hands of all around us every daily cross and trial as if he gave it himself."*[18]

To others she advised: *"[M]any seek to love God by different methods but there is none so short and so easy as to do everything for his love, to set this seal on all our actions, and keep ourselves in his presence by the commerce of our heart with him in full simplicity without embarrassment or disguise."*[19]

"What was the first rule of our dear Savior's life? You know it was to do His Father's Will. Well, then, the first end I propose in our daily work is to do the Will of God; secondly, to do it in the manner He wills it; and thirdly, to do it because it is His will."[20]

Elizabeth encourages us to "use this hallowed setting to spend time considering where God's will might be leading you at this point in your life."

For Reflection

- *"Remember pilgrim, there are no roads, the roads are made by walking" is attributed to Elizabeth Seton. Write in a journal what this statement means for you in your life.*

- *Recall a time when you were thrust into a new role and felt overwhelmed. How did you respond? With this experience to build on, reconstruct the scenario as you would like to have acted. Write a prayer asking God to help you to possess the peace and confidence to act this way the next time such a situation occurs.*

- *Consider Elizabeth's statement, "They do not know what to do with me, but God does." What decisions are you now faced with that require a waiting for "God's blessed time?"*

- *Reflect on what process you use to discern the appropriateness of others' suggestions and guidance during your times of decision making. Pray about whether you are too ready to cede the initiative to others; too fearful to be open to challenge.*

Closing Prayer

Choose one or more of these paired passages from the word of God and from the work of Elizabeth Seton. Ask God to help you cultivate a deeper sensitivity to the ways in which God's will is made manifest in your life.

From the word of God:

Then Mary said, "Here am I, the servant of the Lord; let it be with me according to your word" (Luke 1:38).

From the work of Elizabeth: *All is in his hands. If I had a choice, and my will would decide in a moment, I would remain silent in his hands. Oh, how sweet it is there to rest in perfect confidence.*[21]

From the word of God:

My food is to do the will of him who sent me, and to complete his work (John 4:34).

From the work of Elizabeth:

I keep the straight path to God alone, *the little daily lesson to keep soberly and quietly in his presence, trying to turn every little action on his will, and to praise and love through cloud as sunshine, is all my care and study.*[22]

Notes

[1] Saint Augustine, *Confessions*, trans., R.S. Pine-Coffin (New York: Penguin Classics, 1961), pp. 170, 172.

[2] Elaine M. Prevallet, S.L., "Minding the Call," *Weavings*, Vol. XI, No. 3, May/June 1996, pp. 7-14.

[3] Regina Sigfried and Robert Morneau, eds., *Selected Poetry of Jessica Powers* (Kansas City, Mo.: Sheed and Ward, 1989), p. 19.

[4] Kelly and Melville, p. 189.

[5] Kelly and Melville, pp. 203-204.

[6] Melville, p. 171.

[7] Kelly and Melville, p. 197.

[8] Kelly and Melville, p. 198

[9] Kelly and Melville, p. 234.

[10] Kelly and Melville, p. 262.

[11] Dirvin, *Soul*, p. 40-41.

[12] Dirvin, *Soul*, p. 44.

[13] Kelly and Melville, p. 265.

[14] Kelly and Melville, p. 267.

[15] Dirvin, *Soul*, p. 47.

[16] Ellin Kelly, ed., *Numerous Choirs*, Vol. I (Evansville, Ind.: Mater Dei Provincialate), p. 203.

[17] Kelly, *Numerous Choirs*, p. 218.

[18] Kelly and Melville, p. 303.

[19] Kelly and Melville, p. 357.

[20] Dirvin, *Soul*, p. 51.

[21] Elizabeth Seton to Antonio Filicchi, 8 Feb., 1809, Archives Mount St. Joseph, A 111 053.

[22] Melville, p. 373.

Day Six

'To Speak the Joy of My Soul'

Coming Together in the Spirit

One day a young French country girl, Marguerite Naseau, came to see the great apostle of charity, Vincent de Paul: "Monsieur, I have heard that you need a helping hand. I am not very learned, but I don't spare myself at work.... If you want me, I am ready to serve the poor." She was a cowgirl, and had learned to read while working in the fields, stopping passersby and asking them to help her decipher the letters. Soon she began teaching the village children, and eventually began to move from village to village instructing the young.

When Marguerite approached Vincent with her offer, he said, "Marguerite Naseau...was the first sister to have the happiness of showing the way to others...although she had virtually no other master or mistress than God." Vincent de Paul exhorted his followers, "Let us ask God to give this spirit to the Little Company, the heart of the son of God that motivates us to go out as he would.... He sends us out as he sent his apostles, to carry this fire everywhere, his divine fire, the fire of his love."

While Marguerite lay dying, a victim of her self-sacrifice in sharing her bed with a poor plague-stricken girl, Louise de Marillac was gathering around her others who had resolved to join together in service of the poor. In the imperceptible way in which God works, a new movement had begun, and there was no turning back. These young women willingly went to the outposts of society as the first in a long line of the Company of Charity, carrying the divine fire wherever they were sent.

Defining Our Thematic Context

On Day Five we walked with Elizabeth as God's will unfolded in her willingness to assume unpracticed roles. Her openness created the opportunity for others to serve and be served through the Sisters of Charity she founded. And her reliance on Divine Providence has served as a cornerstone of her community's spirituality as well as a model for many others.

Today we reflect on how Elizabeth's love of God manifested itself in a passionate presence to God Incarnate. Her sense of mission and service, especially to the poor, were characteristics which manifested themselves early in her life and grew in intensity as she matured spiritually. She had a deep desire to serve the poor, but also responded to the needs and practicalities of the situation in which she found herself.

Opening Prayer

Incarnate God, we know that your spirit is a spirit of love which embraces all. In imitation of Jesus during his earthly life, help us to willingly reach out to others even when it is inconvenient or difficult. Teach us to imitate your goodness in welcoming all, and to show great gentleness, compassion and respect, especially to the poor. Imbue us with the knowledge that in serving those in greatest need we are serving you.

Retreat Session Six

Elizabeth is waiting in the quiet of the small "White House" chapel on the grounds at Emmitsburg as we begin to drift in for our gathering. It is a plain room with simple wooden benches and an altar, a place conducive to quiet moments of prayer where little ornamentation stands between the pray-er and God.

After each one has found a place and silence prevails, our mentor arises from her posture of prayer and turns to face us. "I always steal a few extra minutes here when I can," she confides. "This chapel and this building hold such significance for me and for the Sisters of Charity. You see the little classroom across the hall? That is where our service to God's children was born here in the Valley. My companions and I were so happy when we could begin receiving students and orphans here—after all, that's why we came together. Today I want you to breathe in the spirit of these beginnings."

"You know, they say the apple doesn't fall far from the tree," she smilingly comments. "I think in my case that's so true. From my earliest days I had heroes and models of selfless giving within my own family. And their example marked my soul indelibly! Although I don't remember him, I heard many family stories of my minister-grandfather being a particular friend to slaves. He served as catechist to all the African-Americans in New York City and later, at his parish on Staten Island, insisted on integrating his catechumen classes."

Besides her grandfather, Elizabeth was also strongly influenced by her beloved father. Doctor Bayley had a special place in his heart for the poor and outcast. He organized the New York Dispensary for the city's poor and, as health officer of the port of New York, became keenly aware of the plight of Irish immigrants. Elizabeth herself witnessed his selfless ministries to the arriving steerage passengers at the health station on Staten Island. Doctor Bayley was as a father to them, working long hours to alleviate their suffering, eventually becoming a victim of the same fever which was claiming so many of them.

With these examples, is it any wonder that from an early age Elizabeth's heart embraced the world? Without a nod to class, race or nationality, she loved each person as an image of God. To teach, to heal, to gather together, to reconcile were all part of her vision of bringing the world closer to the heart of God. She regarded herself as a "citizen of the world," and wrote, "...*the divine sacrifice so present, the holy holy holy so incessant in the heart—was it then—O my God?—what is distance or separation when our soul plunged in the ocean of infinity sees all in his own bosom—there is nor Europe or America there—our God, and our all...*"[1]

Her missionary desire was to bring God to others both by prayer and action. Elizabeth was a founding member of the Society for Relief of Poor Widows with Small Children, the first benevolent association managed by women in the United States. In this capacity she spent hours visiting the poor, taking them food and clothing, and this while responsible for her own house full of small children. In addition, she and her sister-in-law, Rebecca, eagerly became involved in the outreach work of Trinity Church, giving so much to the poor, sick and dying that their friends came to refer to them as "the Protestant Sisters of Charity."

After establishing the Catholic Sisters of Charity in the United States, opening a school and a parish catechetical program for children (including many people of color), Elizabeth received a donation to *extend the plan to the reception of the aged and also uneducated persons who may be employed in spinning, knitting, etc., etc., so as to found a Manufactory on a small scale which may be very beneficial to the poor.[2]*

Elizabeth's practiced stance of waiting for God's will to unfold in the grace of the moment is expressed to Philip Filicchi:

I have invariably kept in the background and avoided even reflecting voluntarily on anything of the kind knowing that Almighty God alone could effect it if indeed it will be realized. Father Dubourg has always said the same, be quiet God will in his own time discover His intentions, nor will I allow one word of intreaty [sic] from my pen. His blessed will be done.[3]

And yet, as the plan materialized, she poured out her excitement to her friend, Julia Scott, *"to speak the joy of my soul at the prospect of being able to assist the poor, visit the sick, comfort the sorrowful, clothe little innocents and teach them to love God!—there I must stop!"[4]*

By the summer of 1809 Elizabeth and her newly assembled band of Sisters of Charity moved to Emmitsburg, a rural village west of Baltimore, ready to begin their work. Availability to the poor was their first priority, and as Elizabeth told her assembled group, *"We sanctify ourselves for others.... Our name devotes us to their service in any manner that we could truly serve them.... We must display for them the tender compassion of [God's] goodness, be the ministers of [God's] providence for the relief of their miseries, a relief which disposes so well every heart to [God's] better service."[5]*

Their first winter at Emmitsburg was a hard one, however, due to lack of money. It quickly became evident that the community would need to accept boarding pupils to support themselves and their work for the poor. With characteristic flexibility, Elizabeth adapted to this new vision of ministry, and soon there were fifty boarders. She was happy and *at peace...I [was] as a mother encompassed by many children of different dispositions—not all equally amiable or congenial, but bound to love, instruct, and provide for the happiness of all.*[6]

The house filled quickly while additional children waited to be accepted. It was difficult for Elizabeth to turn any away. Her priest-director complained to Bishop Carroll that she "would take the whole country if she could."[7] Day students soon attended St. Joseph's Free School and "St. Joseph's Class" was set up to receive orphans. Opportunities for private instruction were made available for the more talented of this group. Her goal from the start was inclusiveness. Against the advice of her priest-directors, she insisted on making St. Joseph's open to all, including non-Catholics. She reported to a benefactor that they accepted Pennsylvania Dutch or any who trusted in God.

Although Elizabeth's hope *was [for the school] to have been a nursery only for our Saviours [sic] poor country children, but it seems it is to be the means of forming city girls to Faith and piety as wives and mothers.*[8] And she saw this, too, as part of the work God had for her. "*Your little Mother, my darlings, does not come to teach you how to be good nuns or Sisters of Charity,*" she would say plainly, "*but rather I would wish to fit you for that world in which you are destined to live: to teach you how to be good...mothers of families.*"[9]

After Mass on Sunday Elizabeth would seat herself on a small rock near her beloved grotto on St. Mary's Mountain. Here the young Christians would assemble around her for instruction. She related to her dear friend Simon Bruté, "*So many of our mountain children and poor, good Blacks came today for first communion instructions. They were told from the* pulpit, *all to repair to the Sisterhood—so they came as for a novelty but we will try our best...and I have*

all the Blacks...all the blacks for my share to instruct—
excellentissimo!"[10]

Before long Elizabeth was able to send sisters to take
charge of an orphan asylum in Philadelphia. They were
cautioned about dangerous and disagreeable conditions
they would encounter if they accepted this mission, since
war was then being waged with Britain along the Atlantic
coast. Yet the council "unanimously decided that no
personal inconvenience should prevent Sisters of Charity
doing what duty and charity required." Like their work at
Emmitsburg, the ministrations of the sisters were not
confined to the asylum. From the start day pupils
attended classes and soon a free school for German
children was opened. The sisters collected for the poor at
the church door and often visited the sick and indigent.
On Sunday afternoon they visited the alms house, not
only distributing goods but assembling the Catholics for
instructions and preparation for the reception of the
sacraments.

The spread of the sisters' work to Philadelphia and
soon after to New York was a delight to Elizabeth.
Despite declining health, her heart was still ablaze with
zeal. She relished being surrounded by the young people
in her charge, whether the girls from St. Joseph's, the boys
at Mount St. Mary's who always considered her their
mother in a special way, or the neighborhood children in
her catechism classes.

Every moment, I may say, of life, someone is looking to me
to say or do something: sixty and more children boarders,
besides the country children, and treble the Sisters we had when
you were here.

You must give me up, as I do myself, into his Hands Who
has done so much for us both.[11]

But her vision, as ever, was beyond Emmitsburg, to
wherever the gospel could be spread. When her friend

Simon Bruté thought of going with another priest to preach to the Canadian Indians, she exploded with jealousy, "[I]f I was one or the other [of you]! ...I would not stop night or day until I reached the dry and dark wilderness where neither [light nor grace] can be found. O, if I was light and life as you are, I would shout like a madman alone to my God, and roar and groan and sigh and be silent all together until I had baptized a thousand.... In the meantime, that Kingdom come. Every day I ask my bête-soul what I do for it in my little part assigned, and I can see nothing but the smile, caress, be patient, write, pray and WAIT before Him. O...my blessed God, that Kingdom come!"[12]

Elizabeth is flushed with excitement as she recalls the energy and dedication she experiences in her ministry. "I guess you can tell where my heart is!" she comments.

"Whenever I talk about the people I've encountered through my life I get so enthused. I see each one so vividly as a manifestation of God's presence. Echoing Saint Vincent de Paul, I believe that God is so present in those to whom we minister that if we are called to leave prayer to serve others, we are 'leaving God for God.'"

She invites us to explore our apostolic hearts and ask, "Do I allow myself to be touched by God's presence in those most in need?"

For Reflection

- Elizabeth had two wonderful models of service in her grandfather and father. Who were such models for you? Write them letters telling them what their example has meant to you.

- The widow's relief society to which Elizabeth belonged was subject to ridicule and opposition because it was such a *novel idea. Are you aware of projects to help those in need which are subject to ridicule and opposition? Reflect on where you stand in such circumstances.*

- *After one of her visits to a poor widow Elizabeth wrote: "no work, no wood, child sick, etc.—and I should complain, with a bright fire within, bright, bright moon over my shoulder, and the darlings all well...?"*[13] Write a prayer of gratitude for what you have to be most thankful for.

- *"Leaving God for God" has been a formative feature for followers of Vincent de Paul and Elizabeth Seton. Reflect in your journal how this truth could influence your life.*

Closing Prayer:

Choose one or more of these paired passages from the word of God and from the work of Elizabeth Seton. Ask God to implant the fire of love more deeply in your heart and impel you to open-handed response to others.

From the word of God:

> "The Spirit of the Lord is upon me,
> because he has anointed me
> to bring good news to the poor.
> He has sent me to proclaim
> release to captives
> and recovery of sight to the blind,
> to let the oppressed go free,
> to proclaim the year of the Lord's favor" (Luke 4:18).

From the work of Elizabeth: *[T]o speak the joy of my soul at the prospect of being able to assist the poor, visit the sick, comfort the sorrowful, clothe little innocents and teach them to love God!—there I must stop.*[14]

From the word of God:

"Truly I tell you, just as you did it to one of the least of these who are members of my family, you did it to me" (Matthew 25:40).

From the work of Elizabeth: *Does our charity extend to all; is our love for all in our Jesus; do we unite it so closely with Him that life—body and soul—are all devoted to Him?...Do we indeed, give Him the true service of the heart without which whatever else we give has no value?*[15]

Notes

[1] Kelly and Melville, p. 312.

[2] Melville, p. 195.

[3] Melville, p. 195.

[4] Code, p. 183.

[5] Dirvin, *Soul*, pp. 129-130.

[6] Kelly, *Numerous Choirs*, p. 151.

[7] Melville, p. 272.

[8] Kelly and Melville, p. 287.

[9] Dirvin, *Mrs. Seton*, p. 327.

[10] Kelly and Melville, pp. 314, 316.

[11] Dirvin, *Mrs. Seton*, p. 386.

[12] Dirvin, *Soul*, pp. 149-150.

[13] Dirvin, *Soul*, p. 129.

[14] Code, p. 183.

[15] Celeste, p. 105.

Day Seven
'All He Asks of Us Is the Heart'

Coming Together in the Spirit

A Hindu guru and his disciple were traveling from village to village. They walked for several hours during which time they were in deep conversation concerning fundamental questions of life and God. They came upon a river. The guru stopped, guided his disciple to the river and proceeded to hold the disciple's head under the water. He held it there until the disciple began to shake from the inability to breathe. His whole body was calling out for air. Finally, the guru allowed the disciple to come up for air. Raising his head out of the water, the disciple gasped for his breath, for his life. When he finally became calm, he asked his guru, "Why?" The guru responded: "When you want God as much as you wanted air, you will have him."[1]

Defining Our Thematic Context

On Day Six Elizabeth shared with us her apostolic heart. In the tradition of Saint Vincent de Paul, she possessed a passionate sense of God's presence in others, especially the poor. She burned with the zeal of the great missionaries yearning to carry God's word to the far reaches of the earth. Yet she was equally inspired by responding to those who shared her little corner of the world.

Today we will focus on our director's prayer life and how it informed her everyday activities. She relished her time spent in communion with God. She also saw clearly that the activities in which we are engaged, rather than being distractions, bring us nearer to God. These, in fact, become a major way we communicate with God if we but cultivate this awareness.

Opening Prayer

We move so fast, God, and sometimes we see so little in our daily travels. Slow us down. Create in us a desire to pause. Help us to pursue moments of contemplation. Help us to see in a deeper way, to become more aware of what speaks to us of beauty and truth. Amen.

RETREAT SESSION SEVEN

Today we gather at the grotto on St. Mary's Mountain, not far from Elizabeth's valley home of St. Joseph's. It is a wild and picturesque spot where huge rocks overgrown with moss project over a ravine from which a gurgling stream flows. The steep hillside is profuse with vines and wildflowers. "For today, our last day, I've saved the best!" our director greets us. "I want you to breathe our mountain air and taste the repose of the deep woods. It is here that we spend our Sunday afternoons in quiet prayer and sharing. It's my favorite spot!"

Elizabeth settles with obvious pleasure on one of the large boulders that protrude from the earth. We retreatants find comfortable spots around her, eager to share this hallowed space.

Sensing the sacredness of this time, one of the retreatants asks, "Elizabeth, you seem always to be so peace-filled, so able to be in God's presence, to see God's hand in whatever happens. Teach us how to become that way."

With a slight chuckle, Elizabeth pauses, ponders and responds, "Well, it might seem that way to you, but keeping myself rooted in God's loving presence has been a lifelong endeavor. It has to be carefully cultivated and nurtured. And it's something that comes to fuller blossom the more you mature in your prayer life. *Let your chief study be to acquaint yourself with God because there is nothing greater than God, and because it is the only knowledge which can fill the heart with a Peace and joy, which nothing can disturb.*"[2]

From her earliest days Elizabeth felt a "drawing" towards God. The things of the spirit always had a pull for her, they helped her to make sense of her world. Even as a young girl, she delighted in nature and wandered on the shore where *"every little leaf and flower or animal, insect, shades of clouds, or waving trees, [were] objects of vacant unconnected thoughts of God and heaven."*[3]

She loved to care for her younger half-sisters and brothers, reading them prayers and singing hymns over the cradle. In later life, she vividly recalled a profound teenage spiritual experience she enjoyed one May day in the woods:

The air was still, a clear blue vault above, the numberless sounds of spring...[I was] filled with an enthusiastic love of God and admiration for His works.... I thought at the time my father did not care for me—well God was my Father—My All.

I prayed—sung hymns-cryed-laughed in talking to myself of how far HE could place me above all Sorrow—Then layed still to enjoy the Heavenly Peace that came over my Soul and I am sure in the two hours so enjoyed grew ten years in my spiritual life.[4]

But there were other periods too, when her father was gone, and she and her sister, Mary, unwelcome in their father's home, were shuttled to their Uncle Will's. These were lonely and desolate experiences during which she struggled mightily to find God's love in her life. There were also intervals when she was so distracted by the fast pace of life or by intellectual fads that she "could not even say her prayers," and times of near despair when she wondered why God had even created her.

Through the years of her marriage, life was busy with small children and the responsibilities of the household. It sometimes seemed to the young mother that there wasn't one more thing that could be crammed into a day after the sewing, hearing the children's lessons and maintaining her home. She got up early and never went to bed before midnight, and yet reflected: "[T]*here is no greater error than to imagine that the very employments God gives us shall force us to forget Him while we are engaged in them!*"[5] God had given her a great deal to do in those years, but she always hoped to prefer God's will to every wish of her own and begged God to stay with her in her busiest moments.

The future saint had a constant desire to make "*an entire surrender of herself and all her faculties to God,*"[6] and she lived her life in that spirit of "entire surrender." The spiritual journal she kept during this period witnesses to the gift of prayer she was already receiving as a young Episcopalian wife and mother. She wrote of the blessing of the "*power of instant communion with the Father of our spirits, the sense of His presence—the influences of His love.*"[7]

*We must learn to pray literally without ceasing, without
ceasing in every occurrence and employment in our lives...that
prayer which is independent of place or situation, but is rather
a habit of lifting up the heart to God, as in a constant
communication with Him....*[8]

*It is one of the Miracles of Divine Grace and Wisdom that
every state of life which is not reproved by the Law of God may
be referred to our own Salvation—experience daily shows that
the actions which we perform for the discharging of duties of
our state, though they seem sometimes very distracting of
themselves bring US NEARER TO GOD than they remove us
from him—that they augment the desire of his presence and
that He communicates himself to the Soul in such a manner by
secret and unknown ways in the midst of Necessary
distractions that it [God's presence] is never delayed thereby...*

*By carefully elevating our minds to God often in the day—
blessing his holy Name—thanking him for his favors, imploring
his help—speaking to him affectionately—and sighing after the
possession of Him we perpetually entertain the first of Divine
Love—and it frequently happens at these moments that God
will grant what we do not obtain by hours of Prayer to teach us
that it is to his Good we owe Our happiness, more than to our
own care—and that all he asks of US is the Heart.*[9]

Elizabeth cultivated a consistently reflective stance
toward life, and was nurtured by a "latent spring" of
contemplative insight which gave life to all her
endeavors. She did not see engagement and
contemplation as adversaries. Rather, engagement and
contemplation gave energy to each other, held one
another in balance. She strove always to deepen her
understanding of who God is and how God acts by her
daily reflection. Her reflection then moved her to ever
more courageous, responsive and creative efforts on
behalf of others. Transformed by her life of action and
prayer, she acted to change the world according to the

vision of Jesus. She once instructed her sisters:

"If contemplative Magdalenes enjoy more sweetness, they don't possess more merit. One who runs over the whole city carrying God in her thoughts, is more pleasing in God's sight, than another who lets her thoughts run about while they are kneeling in an oratory.... A simple remembrance of the presence of God in us is the starting point. It was particularly recommended by many saints not to exclude the view of God's presence everywhere, but to call our attention to our own interior...God is more within us than we are ourselves."[10]

One of the great blessings of Elizabeth's mature years was the spiritual friendship she enjoyed with Reverend Simon Gabriel Bruté, her "angel of the Mountain." This young French missionary first came to Mount St. Mary's in Emmitsburg for a brief stay in the summer of 1811. While working with him on his English, Elizabeth experienced the beginning of a deep mutuality and lively friendship. Through all Bruté's comings and goings, the two became mentors and directors to each other. The priest's return to Emmitsburg in 1818 as President of Mount St. Mary's was a joy to both of them. They encouraged each other in their enthusiastic dedication to deepening their relationship with God. Bruté's unbounded zeal captivated and inspired the woman he considered his spiritual mother. She tempered his mercurial emotions while helping him soar through his mystical inclinations. At the same time he understood the depth of her spiritual yearnings and was able to guide her during trying times. Each possessed a purity of heart which proved a mutual attraction and spurred the other to deeper holiness.

In one letter Bruté attributed his spiritual growth to her inspiration: "You whom I like to call a mother here, as I call one in France...you have so well helped me better to know, yes better still, a priest of his as I was, to know my happiness and desire, but alas, [I] so vainly desire to impart the same to others to know and love and say Jesus....[11]

Elizabeth in turn referred to him as "Blessed G[abriel]!" and was able to respond to his inspiration as to no other. After rereading material he had shared with her she commented:

"I read again the hundred direction papers of the two years past with yet greater delight than the first reading and gather new courage and stronger faith as when they were first applied—the Grace at present as when they came fresh from the hot press of the burning heart."[12]

During one of his absences she referred to herself as "an old black stump" without the "live coal far away which used to give it the Blaze in a moment."

A volume would not have been enough to say half the heart that fastens to yours more and more if possible—but with such freedom of the local circumstances or position of the moment, that I shall see you go again.... Well, I will see you go to do his will of the present moment with no other signs or desires but for its most full and compleat [sic] accomplishment. Your silly little woman in the fields...your little woman silly of our dear sillyness of prayers and tears, will not hold closer and closer to him who will do all in you, as he does in my poor little daily part and try always to bring you the support of a Mother's prayers, her cry to him for your full fidelity.[13]

And a visit made her realize how much she missed him:

...My son—be most careful to find the Will, not by the dear coaxing your Mother charged you with, but by a prayer of full confidence such as your silly sinner dares to use. From the last look out of the gate I hastened to the dear bench in the choir...to begin this full prayer. To take him by storm G—I will be faithful to it, you know how many times a day and the nights so near him.... But you know the only security and heavenly

*peace is that point so dear rests all on this essential abandon—
so at least you taught me.*[14]

In the last several years of her life, Elizabeth was
blessed to have her soul's companion back in Emmitsburg
again. They continued their ever deepening spiritual
journey, sharing their love and their burdens. Near the
end of her life Elizabeth confided to him, *"Now I think for
every spark of desire I have ever had to love our God and to
show I love, I have a towering flame—but—but—proof you say
poor little soul. Well, blessed, I will try for that too, and I do
beg you in the name of our Eternity to tell me everything I may
do to prove it better."*[15]

Elizabeth witnessed to her privileged awareness of
God's presence in a note to him referring to God as *"Him
from whom I think I have not parted a minute since I saw
you."*[16] And after her death, Brute spoke of the
exceptionally ardent nature of her relationship with God
and likened it to that of the great mystics. He had
affirmed as much in a letter to Elizabeth a few months
before she died, writing that he did not come often to see
her because he did not want to tire her. Besides, he said,
he knew that "the Well-Beloved, the only Spouse of your
soul is continually present. Present in love, confidence,
abandon, the most tender, the most simple, the most
entire abandon."[17]

Always seeking to live closely in God's presence and
to give her heart to her God, Elizabeth lived the advice
she had once given to a friend: Our *"little, daily lesson is to
keep soberly and quietly in God's presence, trying to turn every
little action on His will; and to praise and love through cloud
and sunshine in all cares and study."*[18]

With that, her dark eyes looked intently around the
group of retreatants. "Always in the midst of busy lives
and much activity, we must continually strive to maintain
our interior quiet," she exhorted. "As Christians we are

devoted to the service of others in any way we can truly serve them. We must display for them the tender compassion of God's goodness, be ministers of God's providence for the relief of their needs." But always remember, *[m]any seek to love God by different methods but there is none so sweet and so easy as to do everything for his love, to set this seal on all our actions, to keep ourselves in his presence by the commerce of our heart with him in full simplicity without embarrassment or disguise.*[19]

"Do everything for God's love, keep yourselves in God's presence, in full simplicity, without embarrassment or disguise," she repeats. "Contemplate how you are being asked to give your heart to God amidst your everyday activities. Be prepared to meet your grace in every circumstance of life."

For Reflection

- *What "sacred spot" draws you most deeply into God's presence? Consider how you might visit this place on a regular basis.*

- *Reflect on ways you might "hold on to" God's presence through the fluctuations of events and interior dispositions you experience.*

- *Ask God in your prayer to teach you to "pray literally without ceasing in every occurrence and employment of your life."*

- *Spend time with Elizabeth's expressions of friendship to Simon Bruté. Reflect on a spiritual friendship you enjoy. How does this friendship affect your prayer?*

Closing Prayer

Choose one or more of these paired passages from the word of God and the work of Elizabeth Seton. Ask God to make your prayers heartfelt.

From the word of God:

But you are not in the flesh; you are in the Spirit, since the Spirit of God dwells in you. Anyone who does not have the Spirit of Christ does not belong to him (Romans 8:9).

From the work of Elizabeth: *Our look of love at him draws back a look of love on us, and God's divine look enkindles that fire of love in us which makes us remember him continually.*[20]

From the word of God:

O God, you are my God, I seek you,
my soul thirsts for you;
my flesh faints for you,
...Your steadfast love is better than life (Psalm 63:1, 3).

From the work of Elizabeth: *Think of him, love him, and look to him, and never mind the rest—all will be well.*[21]

Notes

[1] Quoted in Silvio Fittipaldi, *How to Pray Always Without Always Praying* (Liguori, Mo.: Liguori Publications, 1985). From Charles Reutemann, FSC, *Let's Pray/2*, (Bro. Charles Reutemann, FSC, 1982), p. 18.

[2] Kelly and Melville, p. 79.

[3] Kelly and Melville, p. 324.

[4] Kelly and Melville, p. 115.

[5] Dirvin, *Soul*, p. 56.

[6] Kelly and Melville, p. 85.

[7] Dirvin, *Soul*, p. 54.

[8] Dirvin, *Soul*, p. 64.

[9] Kelly and Melville, p. 214.

[10] Dirvin, *Soul*, p. 56.

[11] Melville, p. 295.

[12] Melville, p. 303.

[13] Melville, p. 307.

[14] Melville, pp. 308-309.

[15] Melville, p. 320.

[16] Dirvin, *Soul*, p. 56.

[17] Melville, p. 377.

[18] Dirvin, *Soul*, p. 18.

[19] Kelly and Melville, p. 357.

[20] Dirvin, *Soul*, p. 57.

[21] Elizabeth Seton to Cecilia Seton, 1 July 1807, Archives St. Joseph Provincial House, ASJPH 1-3-3-8:138.

Going Forth to Live the Theme

A kaleidoscope is made up of tiny random bits of colored glass, seemingly meaningless in form. But with a simple turn it reveals beautiful arrangements and patterns. Each design shows itself in an intricate mandala when reflected in the light.

Reflection means bending again, looking anew from a different angle. And, as we watch new patterns come into existence when we turn a kaleidoscope, we are enamored of the beauty and distinctiveness of each pattern.

When we view our everyday lives, often all the little colored chips that make up our experiences seem meaningless and unconnected. They appear to have no form. But if we could reflect, rebend them, looking from a different angle, we would see the beautiful forms they create in the eyes of God in whom they are whole. We would recognize at once the great mandala patterns. We would be aware of the connection of our actions with the larger patterns of God's creation. Without pride in achievement or despair in failure, we would perceive the greater meaning of our lives.[1]

Elizabeth Seton was one who, through varied roles and activities, possessed an ability to appreciate a deeper connection, a deeper meaning. She saw the mandala patterns in her life. Not allowing herself to be pulled mindlessly from one thing to another, she reflectively kept her attention on the overall pattern of God's guiding hand—to the grace of the moment—and let the rest fall where it would.

Our mentor has much to offer us in our efforts to live less scattered lives. We each must find our own ways to develop an awareness of the deeper level to which we are drawn. A great many of our anxieties and problems result from our jumping from one thing to another without so much as drawing a breath. We never become completely present to the thing we are doing as our mind is busily reliving the past or anticipating the future. The reflecting and rebending in search of the beautiful and meaningful must be worked at consciously, little by little, again and again. Sometimes even a short pause and remembering what we are about is enough to bring us to awareness of the present moment and God's presence in it.

As Elizabeth Seton tells us, "We must be so careful to meet our grace—wherever we go there is a store of grace waiting."

Notes

[1] Suggestions for this section come from Helen Luke, *Kaleidoscope* (New York: Parabola, 1992), p. 8.

Deepening Your Acquaintance

The following books, articles and video resources are intended to help you sustain your relationship with Elizabeth Seton. Additional resources are offered for those who want to explore the theme in other contexts.

Books

Alderman, Margaret and Josephine Burns, *Praying with Elizabeth Seton*. Winona, Minn.: Saint Mary's Press, 1992.

Celeste, Sister Marie, *Elizabeth Ann Seton: A Woman of Prayer*. New York: Alba House, 1993.

Dirvin, Joseph I., C.M., *Mrs. Seton*. Emmitsburg, Maryland: Basilica of the National Shrine of St. Elizabeth Ann Seton, 1993.

Dirvin, Joseph I., C.M., *The Soul of Elizabeth Seton: A Spiritual Portrait*. San Francisco: Ignatius Press, 1990.

Kelly, Ellin M., *Elizabeth Seton's Two Bibles: Her Notes and Markings*. Huntington, Ind.: Our Sunday Visitor, Inc., 1977.

Kelly, Ellin M., *Numerous Choirs: A Chronicle of Elizabeth Bayley Seton and Her Spiritual Daughters*. Evansville, Ind.: Mater Dei Provincialate, 1981.

Kelly, Ellin M., and Annabelle Melville, eds., *Elizabeth Seton: Selected Writings*. New York: Paulist Press, 1987.

Melville, Annabelle M., *Elizabeth Bayley Seton*. St. Paul, Minn.: Carillon Books, 1976.

Articles

McNeil, Betty Ann, S.C. "Elizabeth Seton—Mission of Education: Faith and Willingness to Risk," *Vincentian Heritage*, Vol. 17, No. 3, 1996, 185-199.

_____. "Motherhood—Elizabeth Seton's Prism of Faith," *Review for Religious*, November-December, 1994.

Metz, Judith, S.C. "Elizabeth Seton's Founding Community of Sisters of Charity," *U.S. Catholic Historian*.

The entire issue of *Vincentian Heritage*, Vol. XIV, No. 2, is devoted to articles on Elizabeth Seton. Authors include: Regina Bechtle, Mary Ann Donovan, Kathleen Flanagan, Gertrude Foley, Anne Harvey, Ellin Kelly, Judith Metz, Marilyn Thie and Fay Trombley.

Videos

William Nicholson with Joss Ackland and Claire Bloome, *A Time For Miracles*, American Broadcasting Company (Los Angeles: Charter Entertainment, 1986).